Five Indian Novelists

The Self, the Family and Society
in
Five Indian Novelists

Rajan, Raja Rao, Narayan, Arun Joshi, Anita Desai

V.V.N. Rajendra Prasad

PRESTIGE

Published by
Prestige Books
3/28, East Patel Nagar, New Delhi 110 008
in association with
Indian Society for Commonwealth Studies
New Delhi

ISBN: 81-85218-27-7

Jacket design by
3-A Corporation,
New Delhi 110 002

Phototypesetting by
data culture
New Delhi 110 065
Ph. 6431070

Printed at
Mehra Offset Press
New Delhi 110 002

Contents

To
My Mother

Preface

A critical evaluation of contemporary creative writings has its own advantages and disadvantages. Given the cultural, intellectual, and academic climate of opinion that has been prevailing in the study of Indian Writing in English, it is not easy to evolve a viable and valid criterion of critical assessment. Exclusive and absolute formalism may compel a critic to ignore the cultural matrix that has made the Indian novel in English possible. On the other hand, a complete disregard for the formal considerations of the Indian Novel in English may convert any critical assessment into a documentary review of creative writing which deserves to be considered creative writing. In short, a reassessment of contemporary creative writing ought to be a happy fusion of the claims of art and the claims of relevance. A study of the self, the family, and society in the novelists under review seems to be a pragmatic, if not a scientifically exact, critical approach, in the sense that it helps us explore the themes of the writers and their creative articulation.

The Indian novelists who constitute the subject of this study have been active practitioners of the form. Since the short-story in Indian writing in English may be considered an autonomous field of enquiry in itself, I am constrained to focus my attention exclusively on the novel--the novels of Rajan, Raja Rao, Narayan, Arun Joshi, and Anita Desai.

I am deeply indebted to my teacher Professor A. Ramakrishna Rao, Chairman, Board of Studies in English, Sri Krishnadevaraya University, Anantapur, whose scholarly advice and criticism have been of immense help to me. I thank all my colleagues in the department for the prompt help rendered on various occasions. My thanks are due to the UGC and the authorities of Sri Krishnadevaraya University for the grant of subsidy for the publication of this book. I wish to place on record my thankfulness to Dr. R.K. Dhawan, University of Delhi, for encouraging me to publish my thesis. I have a great pleasure in thanking Prestige Books for so elegantly bringing out this book.

If you continue to speak well of narrative it follows
that you will speak well of the novel.

Frank Kermode

The Indian Novel in English: Its Socio-Cultural Milieu

I

K.R. Srinivasa Iyengar begins his survey of the Indian novel in English with the assertion that "The 'novel' as a literary phenomenon is new to India."[1] Although there was a rich narrative tradition in Sanskrit and in other Indian languages, the novel as a literary form had its origin in the "literary renaissance" that swept Bengal in the later half of the nineteenth century. Inspired by the social revolution against some of the deplorable practices in Hindu society, Bankim Chandra Chatterjee (1838-1894) dramatizes the plight of characters caught in the rigour and rigidity of Hindu joint families. Tagore, in his novel *Binodini (Choker Bali)*, dramatizes the psychological tension of a young widow who confronts a hostile society when she tries to assert herself as a woman. Sarat Chandra Chatterjee, in a series of novels, tries to acclimatize the Indian mind to the uses of realism. In the southern parts of India there was an equally vigorous and fervent social criticism against the economic exploitation, the rigidity of the caste system, and the miserable condition of young widows in society. Most of the criticism took the form of sarcastic essay. The spread of the English language and education in India brought the Indian mind into a happy contact with the Victorian novel. In any literary discussion, the word "influence" is a misleading term, and tracing literary influence may turn into a vague and slippery enterprise. To quote Iyengar, "Before 1947 (the year of the withdrawal of Britain's political connection), the English models were the major outside influence on the Indian novel. After independence, however, novelists in India have shown themselves susceptible to the influence of American and European (especially Russian) models, and also models from Oriental countries."[2] Discussing the thematic complex of the Indian novel in English, Iyengar says, "After the advent of independence, the more serious novelist has shown how the joy of freedom has been more than neutralized by the tragedy of the 'partition'; how in spite of the freedom there is continuing (or even galloping) corruption, inefficiency, poverty and cumulative misery; how, after all, the mere replacement of the white sahib by the brown sahib cannot effect a radical cure for the besetting ills of India. When independence came, the serious novelist in a sense found his occupation gone, for the traditional villain of the piece—foreign rule—was no more in the picture. Making a new start as it were, the novelist shifted his lantern this side and that, made his probes, and found little to satisfy him. The old narrow loyalties were seen to wax as eloquent as ever. Communal, linguistic, casteist passions were seen to come into the open with accelerated frequency."[3]

The sociology of the Indian novel in English is a problematic subject, in the sense that it cannot be established by taking into account the conflicts that crop up between various classes. Hindu society is not meaningful in terms of Marxian ideology. Terms like "bourgeois" and "proletariat" do not illuminate the struggles and tensions which Hindu society has been subjected to since times immemorial. Moreover, the sociological landscape in India during British rule doesn't suggest any contrast between a city and a village. We don't come across in the regional literatures novels exclusively preoccupied with human problems in a metropolis like the novels of Balzac, Dostoevsky, Dickens, Thackeray, Flaubert, Zola, and Dreiser. The obvious reason appears to be that both in the city and in the country the significant classification of the population is on the principle of caste and community. People who do menial jobs are segregated to a separate area outside the city or the village. When Gandhi entered the socio-political scene during the thirties, it was this section of Indian society that had attracted his attention. Inspired by Gandhi, creative artists in various Indian languages brought to a central focus the sociological and the psychological problems of untouchables whom Gandhi rechristened *Harijans*. Making use of the conventions of realism as they evolved in Victorian and Edwardian England, the Indian novelist in English has drawn the attention of the international community to the Indian socio-cultural landscape. Before we proceed further in graphing the Indian novel in English and its socio-cultural milieu, it is desirable to discuss the conventions of literary realism in the Indian context. Indian imagination, nourished on the heroic mode we have in the epics and the erotic epyllions of the middle ages, understands and dramatizes life in terms of the ideal norms of human behaviour and conduct. This imagination was exposed to Western literary realism in the middle of the nineteenth century and since then it has preoccupied itself with the burning social issue of the times, such as untouchability, casteism, opposition to British rule, and harassment of orphans and young widows. In a few exceptional cases, it successfully tackles the problem of miscegenation, as exemplified in Tagore's novel *Gora*. "Middle-distance" realism as formulated by J.P. Stern, it may be safely stated, is new to the Indian mind, and we notice its manifestation only in the thirties of the present century. Stern says that realism of the middle distance cannot be given an accurate description or a scientific definition. It is a combination of meaning, fact, and language, and is inseparably connected with the purpose of the whole work which employs it. In a very illuminating passage, he says, "After all, 'the purpose of the whole,' or again 'the proper point of perspective' that determines the middle distance of realism, is the most familiar thing in all literature; it is the fictional creation of *people*, of individual characters and lives informed by what in any one age is agreed to constitute a certain integrity and coherence. ('An age' is no more than a community of agreements in time.) Moreover, the integrity and coherence that realism requires is present in the raw material as well as in the finished product; that is, in the persons and the world to which the realist directs his interest as well as in 'the characters' and 'the world' which he 'recreates' in the pages of his fiction. If literary realism is inseparably related to realism outside literature, then its fictional creations must 'match and make' a world in which the realistic attitude (in its 'real-life' meaning) makes sense. And this attitude in turn only makes sense and works (that is, makes a meaningful difference to things) in a world in which there are *people*, individuals of some degree of integrity and coherence of character."[4]

II

Mulk Raj Anand is the first Indian novelist to make use of middle-distance realism—as formulated by Stern—in his minor classic, *Untouchable*. He dramatizes the activities of a day in the life of a scavenger—the "low-caste" boy, Bakha. The locale and the society of *Untouchable* conform to the canons of realism, in the sense that scavengers and sweepers are pariahs in a society dominated by obsolete and outworn caste morality. Since the town Bulashah has a military cantonment, the army personnel, who include a few Englishmen also, are a part and parcel of the society in which Bakha moves and does his work. The Tommies (the Englishmen, as they are humorously called) and a few Christian missionaries have no reservations about Bakha, though their attitude is one of petty condescension. It is definitely better than the attitude of the Hindus of the higher castes. When the novel was published in 1935, most Indians must have recognized the significance of Bakha. Mulk Raj Anand, exploiting the tensions in Indian society, makes the reader see for himself the poverty, suffering, sincerity, and humanity of the sweeper boy. Adhering to the point of view of Bakha, the novelist makes the reader realize for himself the viciousness and villainy of the caste Brahmins who try to dishonour Bakha's sister, Sohini; and her innocence is clearly contrasted with the corruption of the Brahmins in the temple. Mulk Raj Anand is not unaware of the social change that has taken place with Gandhi's entry into the Indian social scene. Gandhi fervently argued and demanded that the Bakhas of India should find a place in the Indian temple. In fact, in the novel, we see Gandhi addressing a public meeting. The very fact that Bakha hears Gandhi expressing his views on the privileges of *Harijans* in society amply demonstrates the significance of Anand's inaugural and innovatory novel.

Raja Rao's *Kanthapura*, published in 1938, may be construed as a variation on the theme of untouchability. While Mulk Raj

Anand dramatizes the theme from the point of view of a *Harijan* sweeper boy placed in an urban society, Raja Rao shows how a Brahmin boy has to encounter prejudice and callousness in order to make a rural community realize the social injustice to which they are utterly indifferent. The kind of realism we have in *Kanthapura* is a good illustration of the way in which an Indian novelist in English acclimatizes it to the Indian conditions. As Stern rightly observes, "Early sociologists came to insist that the individual self, in any living sense, *even as a self*, is already inextricably involved in a social whole. They were thus re-establishing a unity and a truth which the realistic artists had never ceased to take for granted."[5] Anand and Raja Rao, the "realistic artists," noticed the divisions in Indian society and realized that the Gandhian revolution is the only solution to achieve social integration.

It may be safely asserted that most Indian artists have creatively exploited the socio-political changes that came over India during the Independence struggle. The images of Gandhi we see in R.K. Narayan's *Waiting for the Mahatma*, K.A. Abbas's *Inqilab*, and Chaman Nahal's *The Crown and the Loincloth* suggest that literary realism explores new areas of worldly experience as and when they become accessible to the creative artist. Khushwant Singh's *Train to Pakistan*, Rajan's *The Dark Dancer*, Malgonkar's *A Bend in the Ganges*, and Chaman Nahal's *Azadi* are a creative comment on the problems and the chaotic conditions that defaced India after the Partition. Yet another prolific theme that the Indian novel in English has explored is the East-West encounter. Discussing this aspect of the Indian novel in English, Rajan observes, "India today is facing radical challenges not merely in its sociological landscape but perhaps even in that immemorial landscape of the heart. The clash is not simply between East and West (a conventional but deceptive stylization) but between the *mores* of a pre-urban civilization and one committed to drastic industrial growth. The question to be answered is whether the Indian tradition with its capacity for assimilation and its unique power of synthesis can come to terms with the new (and the new is the inevitable) without deep erosions in its fundamental character. In creating an image of this challenge there is perhaps a part to be played by the man of mixed sensibility, caught between crossfires, whose own mind is a microcosm of what he seeks to convey."[6] Rajan, a "man of mixed sensibility, caught between crossfires, whose own mind is a microcosm of what he seeks to convey," conveys a significant ambivalence in *The Dark Dancer*, in which his protagonist, Krishnan, finds the West attractive but unsteady and the East unattractive but compelling. Most Indian novelists make the East-West encounter profound and pervasive, with various degrees of achievement and success. In the chapters on the individual authors, we discuss this aspect of the Indian novel in English. Suffice it to say here that this theme in and by itself has not produced a memorable novel. When this theme is fused with other themes like communal disharmony and quest for identity, it acquires richness and complexity.

III

Robert Nisbet, in his *Sociology as an Art Form*, says, "At the center of any given style lies what can only be called a theme, or a cluster of themes. Theme carries with it a more active, positive, and dynamic character than does the word style. Implicit in any theme is at once a question being answered, more or less, and also an ordering of experience and observation in a special focus."[7] Nisbet thinks that terms like "realism," "naturalism," "Romanticism," and "classicism" may be construed as various styles of thinking and working. A critical consideration of Narayan's novels from the point of view of theme as a method of the "ordering of experience and observation in a special focus" would make them an important sub-genre in the Indian novel in English. His Malgudi stories emerge from a view of life in which discrimination and sagacity are disciplined and controlled by kindness and reverence for life. Most of his characters come from lower middle-class families and suffer from all the foibles flesh is heir to. Without using the sophisticated and complex rhetoric of fiction, Narayan conveys the charm of social institutions like the family, marriage, property, worship, and yoga. His novels and stories implicitly pose the question whether human beings are using them or abusing them, and in either case, with what consequences. In the novels, there is no explicit answer to this question. We do not come across in Narayan any tragic event that has a devastating effect on life. In most of his stories, we notice a melodramatic turn or twist in the lives of the characters, which leaves them chastened and secure. The point may be illustrated by analyzing Narayan's *The Dark Room*, published in 1938, and by comparing it with Anita Desai's *Where Shall We Go This Summer?*, published in 1975. In both the novels, marriage and marital harmony and disharmony are brought to a central focus from different perspectives. Savitri and Sita, in spite of their sincere efforts to assert their own rights as wives and women, ultimately return home not to please their husbands but to play a role and fulfil an obligation in a network of social relations. Narayan's couple, Savitri and Ramani, suffer a temporary separation, because of Raman's fascination for and relationship with Shanta Bai, an assistant in the insurance office where he is the boss. Having quarrelled with her husband over the issue, Savitri leaves the house. She reaches the banks of the Sarayu and tries to commit suicide by drowning in the river, but Mari, a bad character, who lives on the other side of the river, rescues her and leaves her on the sands. His wife, Ponni, takes her to her huts. She tells Savitri, "Sister, remember this. Keep the men under the rod, and they will be all right. Show them that you care for them and they will tie you and treat you like a dog."[8] Ponni's technique of keeping "the men under the rod" may be a practicable proposition among the lower castes but very difficult to practise among the families of the higher castes. Savitri, after much struggle, returns home to perform her duty as a Hindu wife and to fulfil her obligation to her children as their mother. The narrator's comment on Ramani's embarrassing position unmistakably suggests the signification of *The Dark Room:*

> Ramani got up from the bed after a night of disturbed sleep. With all his bravado before his wife, he was very much shaken by her manner. Such a thing had never happened to him at any time for fifteen years. She had always been docile and obedient, and the fire inside her was a revelation to him now. Though he had invited her to walk out of the house last night, he had not expected her to do it. He had expected she would

> go into the dark room and sulk for a few days, a few days more than usual; then she was bound to come to her senses and accept things as they were. He felt irritated when people made any fuss. A man had a right to a little fun now and then, provided it didn't affect his conduct at home. No doubt it took him home rather late, but that could have been rectified by a little persistent persuasion on her part, all this sullenness and dictation was not the right way to set about it; he expected to be coaxed and requested; he told himself that people could get anything from him if only they knew the proper way of approaching him. It would be a very bold person indeed who tried to dictate to him. (91-92)

Since times immemorial, a dark room has special significance in the wife-husband relationship. Depending on the caste and the status of the family, a woman seeks the consolation of a dark room whenever her husband wounds her feelings or turns recalcitrant. When Ramani tells his wife, "What a dutiful wife!" Would rather starve than precede her husband: You are really like some of the women in our ancient books," (13) it may sound ironical, but there are, even in contemporary India, wives who do not take food till their husbands take it. Even today most wives take it as a compliment if they are told that they are like the women in the ancient books. William Walsh thinks that "*The Dark Room* is the account of marriage given throughout from the point of view of the wife, in which the image projected is that of the Indian woman as a victim, written, it should be remembered, some thirty-five to forty years before the current talks of women's liberation."[9] If we read Anita Desai's *Where Shall We Go This Summer?*, written and published three decades after *The Dark Room*, at a time when women's liberation is not a programme but a reality, we can notice that Sita is in no way a more sophisticated and liberated woman than Narayan's Savitri. Though the narrative is routed through the consciousness of Sita, and the chronology is collapsed in order to facilitate a composite vision of Sita and her familial life, as a daughter and as a wife, we find that her revolt is against the structural compulsions of a society in which the image of woman has not changed since the publication of *The Dark Room*.

"Part One/Monsoon'67" dramatizes Sita's visit to Manori, a village situated on an island near Bombay. Fed up with the business atmosphere of Bombay and nursing a grouse against her husband, who is "not an introvert, nor an extrovert—a middling kind of man, he was dedicated unconsciously to the middle way,"[10] Sita, accompanied by two of her children, goes to the island in order not to give birth to a fifth baby. Her father, a Gandhian, had built a huge structure in the village and stayed there till the end of his life, doing social service to the village folk. The villagers worshipped him as he had performed miracles. Sita goes to the village house on her pilgrimage, fondly hoping that she can miraculously keep the baby in her womb unborn. Unlike Ramani in Narayan's novel, Sita's husband, Raman, appears to be sensible and conducts himself in such a way that he doesn't want to lose his place in the Bombay society. "Part II/Winter'47" presents, in a flashback, Sita's father and his saintly life in the village. But we learn that Sita's mother had left her (Sita's) father and children and was supposed to have stayed in Benares for twenty years. Sita learns from her brother, Jivan, that her mother, unable to live with her husband, whom everybody called a second Gandhi, ran away to Benares. Curiously enough, Sita doesn't find any clue regarding the mystery that surrounds her mother and her flight in a biography of her father written by an old lady. After her father's death, his friend's son, Raman, becomes her guardian and her husband. Although Sita follows Raman, she doesn't appear to be highly grateful to Raman for his timely help. She feels: "It was as though he had been expressly sent by providence to close the theatrical era of her life, her strange career, and lead her out of the ruined theatre into the thin sunlight of the ordinary, the everyday, the empty and the meaningless."(100) "Part Three/Monsoon '67" brings the wife and husband together. Raman goes to the village and Sita thinks that he has come to take her home. Although she has many reservations about her husband and her children, Sita feels "comfort, security, and dull, safe routine walk in, in quiet, grey strides. She remembered it was the second time he had come to fetch her from the island that he was always having to save her from the island."(130-31) But she is mildly shocked when her husband tells her that he has come to take their daughter Menaka, so that she may join the medical college. In spite of her anguish that she is betrayed by her own daughter and in spite of her unarticulated protest against her husband's view of life, she accompanies her husband and the children to the city. Although Sita appears more spirited and shows a greater awareness of the kind of life that is possible for a woman in the changing society of contemporary India than Narayan's Savitri, she also has to toe the line of her husband just for saving the family.

Narayan's limpid prose and Anita Desai's lyrical prose converge on an identical theme, of which the dark room and the island are the controlling metaphors. Among the Indian novelists in English, there are not many who have tried to experiment with form as such. In Arun Joshi and Anita Desai, we have characteristics of the modernist novel. Their novels may be called introverted novels, in the sense that they show an "awareness of the ephemerality and discontinuity of modern reality, of the evanescence of character, the disorderly sequence of time,"[11] which are the special features of the introverted novel in the Anglo-American literature of the twenties and thirties.

IV

In selecting novelists to support his thesis and substantiate his argument, the author is guided by a few obvious norms. The fictional terrain has to be such that it is a fusion of the claims of relevance and the claims of art. The five novelists whose work is under a critical review in the following pages have structured their imaginative insights in such a way that they serve both as a mirror and as a lamp. The images of society that are reflected in these writers are complex and unified. But it must be reiterated that we don't read these writers in order to forge a sociology of the Indian novel in English. We go to them to appreciate the way in which they successfully function as lamps, that is, for the light they throw on the Indian socio-cultural problematic. Moreover, as Joan Rockwell rightly says, "fiction is not only a representation of social reality, but also a necessary functional part of social control, and also paradoxically an important element in social change. It plays a large part in the socialization of infants, in the expression of official norms such as law and religion, in the conduct of politics, and in general gives symbols and modes of life to the population, particularly in those less easily defined but basic areas such as norms, values, and personal and interpersonal behaviours.''[12] Even a casual reader of Kamala Markandaya's novels may see that the narrative focus in her novels is on the stress and strain to which the masses in rural India expose themselves. *Nectar in a Sieve, A Handful of Rice, The Coffer Dams,* and *Pleasure City* foreground the sort of socio-cultural milieu we have in Mulk Raj Anand's *Untouchable, Coolie, Two Leaves and a Bud, The Village, Across the Black Waters,* and *The Sword and the Sickle.* By considering these novels from the point of view of the sociology of the novel embodied in Joan Rockwell's observation cited earlier—it may be positively stated—we get a faithful image of the socio-cultural norms that prevail in contemporary India. But a sensible reader of a novel would generally expect that the image of society the novel dramatizes is the result of a creative synthesis of the cause and the effect that are there in any fictional situation. Though she is a prolific writer, Kamala Markandaya's fiction sometimes doesn't succeed in fusing analysis and action, and so when one reads it, one gets the feeling that ''If the outer theme of *Nectar in a Sieve* was rural economics, the theme of *A Handful of Rice* is urban economics.''[13] Although the foregoing classification doesn't do justice to a competent novelist, the fact that her fiction lends itself to this kind of classification (''rural economics'' and ''urban economics'') suggests that it falls short of achieving the kind of success that is possible. Ruth Prawer Jhabvala has written a series of novels, dramatizing the socio-cultural landscape of New Delhi. She doesn't form a part of this thesis because the sensibility that shapes her fiction is largely European. Hence Anita Desai becomes an obvious choice. A rapid review of her maiden novel, *Cry, the Peacock,* would reinforce the point. Maya marries Gautama for the simple reason that she sees a sort of resemblance between Gautama and her father. After her marriage she feels restless and miserable because everybody in Gautama's house seems to neglect her. The following passage very well illustrates Maya's obsessive thinking:

> "No one, no one else," I sobbed into my pillow as Gautama went into the bathroom, "loves me as my father does." The curtain fell behind him, in tragic folds. He did not hear me—the tap was running. The vacuum into which I spoke made me more frantic, and yet he was not really meant to hear. In Gautama's family one did not speak of love, far less of affection. One spoke—they spoke—of discussions in Parliament, of cases of bribery and corruption revealed in government, of newspaper editors accused of libel, and the trials that followed, of trade pacts made with countries across the seas, of political treaties with those across the mountains, of distant revolutions, of rice scarcity and grain harvests. . . . They had innumerable subjects to speak on, and they spoke incessantly. Sometimes, in order to relax, they played games of cards, so swiftly, so nervously, so intently, that they found they had to release the mounting pressure by conversing, and would begin to talk again, of political scandal and intellectual dissent.[14]

Given the preoccupations of Gautama's family, it is not hard to surmise that Maya is a misfit in that family. Moreover, as she had her father completely to herself, Maya would like to have Gautama completely to herself. The situation is complicated further by the astrological prediction that her husband will predecease her. With all these oppressive thoughts arraigning her mind, Maya, in a moment of utter disagreement with her husband, argues with him and causes his fall from a building which is not protected by a parapet.

This brief summary of the novel doesn't convey the rich texture of Anita Desai's fictional text. But it suggests a significant point. The heroine's name, Maya, is very suggestive and symbolic. In the Hindu Vedantic tradition, *Maya* doesn't mean what is unreal, it only means a lower kind of reality as contrasted with a higher kind of reality. Together they constitute what we see and perceive in the phenomenal world. Maya is in a state of *Maya* because she thinks that nobody loves her except her father. In Indian joint families it is not always easy and possible for a young husband to remind his wife constantly that he loves her. If one keeps this in mind and reads the novel, it is possible to assess not only the creative insight in the novel but also its social insight. The sort of privacy Maya wants to have with her husband also demonstrates the changing views about a family. Joint families deny privacy and may impose regimentation, which choke and stifle the Mayas of Indian society. Anita Desai employs psycho-narration to unravel Maya's hopes, fears, obsessions, and the tragic melancholy we notice in her. A later chapter in the book discusses Anita Desai's fiction not only in terms of her art but in terms of her major thematic concerns and the images that solidify them. The solidity of specification we come across in Anita Desai's novels reveals the subtle interrelationship between the self, the family, and society. Although she uses modernist narrative methods, her narratives are rooted in the problematic of woman and society in a very inclusive sense.

V

F.R. Leavis, in "Sociology and Literature," says: "It is an elementary point, but one that seems unlikely to get too much attention as the Sociology of Literature forges ahead: No 'sociology of literature' and no attempt to relate literary studies with sociological will yield much profit unless informed and controlled by a real and intelligent interest—a first-hand critical interest—in literature."[15] In the chapters that follow, the analysis of the individual novels proceeds by giving maximum attention to the narrative modes embodied in a fictional text. The sociological aspects of the novels as suggested by the title "Self, Family, and Society" emerge as a by-product of the narrative analysis. The Leavisian observation on sociology and literature is kept in view throughout the study, so that the explication of the theme— "self, family, and society"—may not go beyond the confines of what is literary. Adapting the conventions of Anglo-American realism to the Indian context, the novelists of this study have dramatized some of the contemporary socio-cultural issues which have their origin in the nature of the Indian society, and sometimes in India's past. A keen student of Indian society may notice two significant strains in contemporary Indian thought. One may be called transcendental, the other, humanistic.[16] The transcendental aspect of Indian thought is enshrined in the ancient and the medieval Sanskrit literature, including the *Vedas*, the epics, the *Puranas*, and the commentaries on them. The humanistic tradition has its origin in the socio-cultural revolution—a concomitant of the freedom struggle—that swept India during the later half of the nineteenth century. In the novelists of this study, we find the dual perspectives of Indian thought fused and dramatized, with varying degrees of achievement. The images of India we see in the novels are closely connected, because of the rich and significant way in which they illuminate the problems of the self, the family, and society.

NOTES

1. K.R. Srinivasa Iyengar, *Indian Writing in English*, (New Delhi: Sterling, rev. ed., 1984), p.314.
2. *Ibid.*, p. 319.
3. *Ibid.*, pp. 319-20.
4. J.P. Stern, *On Realism* (London: Routledge and Kegan Paul, 1973), p. 121. Malcolm Bradbury says that "middle-distance" realism is "a form of address to the material and the reader which feels no need to assert by verbal or modal self-consciousness that it is basically a construct of words and perspectivized distances." *Possibilities: Essays on the State of the Novel* (London: Oxford University Press, 1973), p. 19.
5. J.P. Stern, p. 101.
6. Balachandra Rajan, "Identity and Nationality," *Commonwealth Literature: Unity and Diversity in a Common Culture,* ed. John Press (London: Heinemann Educational Books, 1965); rpt. in *Considerations*, ed. Meenakshi Mukherjee (New Delhi: Allied, 1977), p. 3.
7. Robert Nisbet, *Sociology as an Art Form* (New York: Oxford University Press, 1976), p. 31.
8. R.K. Narayan, *The Dark Room* (New Delhi: Orient Paperbacks,

1977), p. 90.

9. William Walsh, *R.K. Narayan: A Critical Appreciation* (New Delhi: Allied, 1983), p. 43.
10. Anita Desai, *Where Shall We Go This Summer?* (Delhi: Orient Paperbacks, 1982), p. 47.
11. John Fletcher and Malcolm Bradbury, "The Introverted Novel," in Malcolm Bradbury and James McFarlane, ed., *Modernism: 1890-1930, Pelican Guide to European Literature* (Harmondsworth: Penguin Books, 1976), p. 411.
12. Joan Rockwell, *Fact in Fiction: The Use of Literature in the Systematic Study of Society* (London: Routledge and Kegan Paul, 1974), p. 4.
13. K.R. Srinivasa Iyengar, p. 445.
14. Anita Desai, *Cry, the Peacock* (Delhi: Orient Paperbacks, 1983), pp. 46-47.
15. F.R. Leavis, "Sociology and Literature," *The Common Pursuit* (1952; rpt. Harmondsworth: Penguin Books, 1976), p. 198.
16. V.K. Gokak discusses this aspect in "The Transcendental and Humanistic Traditions," *The Concept of Indian Literature* (New Delhi: Munshiram Manohar Lal, 1979), pp. 117-24.

Rajan and the Ambivalent Self

In Rajan's *Too Long in the West*, the American professor who has to guide Nalini's studies in Columbia University tells her, "My dear girl . . . before you can really learn anything, you must first learn how to learn. Your mind isn't a sponge, mopping up information. It ought to be a kind of light, shining into the facts and revealing their pattern. Look after your intelligence and learn to use it responsibly. It's the little core of difference that makes you yourself. If you didn't own it, then everything else would own you."[1] The professor's advice to Nalini contains in an embryonic form the thematic complex of Rajan's two novels. The usual response to *The Dark Dancer* and *Too Long in the West* has been in terms of the critical cliches like the East-West encounter, the problem of identity, the discovery of the self, and the multifaceted reality dramatized as a tension generated by conflicting value systems. A careful scrutiny of the novels seems to suggest that Rajan's protagonists are preoccupied with the problematic of learning, which is a responsible activity. In the passage just cited, the crucial word appears to be the verb "learn." The entire activity of learning consists in one having a firm hold on one's intelligence. How meaningful the idea "If you didn't own it, then everything else would own you" is can be elucidated by focusing attention on the organization of the two novels.

The Dark Dancer and *Too Long in the West* are foregrounded in South-Indian culture, which has a few special traits. The influence of Western manners and morals hasn't penetrated deeply into South-Indian society. By no stretch of imagination could it be called cosmopolitan. *The Dark Dancer* dramatizes the journey of a South-Indian Brahmin from irresponsible use of intelligence to an awareness of intellectual responsibility. The fictional device that makes the journey possible is the institution of "arranged marriage." In *Too Long in the West,* this device takes the form of a parody which brings home the significance of the idea of using intelligence responsibly.

In *The Dark Dancer,* Krishnan's evolution to selfhood is facilitated by the communal clashes that devastated the country just before and after Independence. Khushwant Singh's *Train to Pakistan,* Malgonkar's *A Bend in the Ganges,* and Chaman Nahal's *Azadi* converge on the turbulent times, one of the plot items in Rajan's novel. Even a superficial reading of these novels would make it obvious that the Hindu-Muslim conflict in Rajan's novel is just a plot-device and not the core of it.

The most crucial event in the narrative is the priest's inability to bless Krishnan and Cynthia when they visit Lord Krishna's temple in Mutthra. Although Krishnan tries to avoid his intellectual confusion by saying that "Wherever a Brahmin is, there is a temple,"[2] the confusion almost amounts to a spiritual/nervous breakdown. He tells Cynthia:

> Rejection by the family, by other people, by society, is one thing. One expects it automatically and is prepared to meet it. But this was so much deeper. It was so deep that I had forgotten my defenses." (169)

When Cynthia taunts him that he has been too religious to take things lightly, he says:

> It'sn't religion. It's just something deeper than society or the family. You take it for granted until you realize that it'sn't available. That's what happened to me. It never struck me that I'd have to do without it. Never, until I looked into the priest's eyes. And then I knew what it was. After I'd lost it, of course." (169-70)

The above passages unmistakably demonstrate the sense of loss that oppresses Krishnan. If we make a short review of his career up to this point, a few clues will emerge and help us in noticing the integration of the self, the family, and society in *The Dark Dancer*. Krishnan's homecoming has the significance one normally notices in any fiction that tries to dramatize the feelings of one who was away from home for a long time. It is a re-entry into a society dominated by traditional forms of family reunions. His parents and his uncles expect him to contribute to the stability and security of their home. Arrangements are set afoot to convert him into a bridegroom, so that he can become an integral part of the family. The family has its ancestral house in the Nungambakam area of Madras, where festivals like *Deepavali* are celebrated with pomp. His marriage with Kamala, an arranged marriage, doesn't create any sense of belonging in Krishnan's mind. From start to finish, Kamala's composure, detachment, and her traditional attitude as a Hindu wife do not make any appreciable impression on him. He feels that "She would not change him. She would accept him. She would leave him nothing but himself, no mask, no pretence, no illusion. Without harshness, perhaps without love also, she would lead him to the precipice of belonging, the point of no return and no escape." (19) In the passage cited above, the emphasis seems to be on the traditional Hindu marriage view, according to which the bride simply accepts the groom. This idea is reinforced by the following passage:

> A servant had opened the twice-bolted wooden gate, and the car drove slowly into the portico, the tyres crunching on the loose gravel. Krishnan's father greeted them almost perfunctorily. His mother embraced them, but a little abstractedly, as if her emotions were elsewhere. For them the climax was over. Now the consequences had to be measured and sifted, a structure of responsibilities modified, a new member integrated into the light, *almost ruthless hierarchy of the family. Had it really been Krishnan and Kamala that mattered?* Or was it their marriage, satisfying Father's resolve to *manoeuver his son into his proper station, satisfying Mother's inarticulate longing for prestige, Kruger's lust for antiquity* and the common hunger for significant spectacle? The multi-

colored cloth of festivity was gone now and there remained only the pretexts on which it hung.[6] (Emphasis added)

The above crucial passage brings to a central focus the multiple plot-lines that reach their culmination in Kamala's death. Krishnan and Kamala have to be incorporated into the "ruthless hierarchy of the family." The family seems to value status, position, spectacle, and festivity. The bride and the bridegroom appear to be pawns that could be manoeuvred on the marital chess-board. The newly married couple have more awareness of their position and privilege in the family hierarchy and less awareness of what they are to each other. This inference appears to be plausible if we analyze his attitude to and participation in the non-cooperation movement. Krishnan doesn't repose any confidence in non-violent resistance to the police brutality. When Vijayaraghavan is thrashed by the police, Krishnan loses his temper and gives a hard hit to a policeman. As the narrator comments, "Krishnan felt the liberation dwelling in him also. It was the natural way to change a problem—the hammer of force and not the mirror of protest."[7] The hammer and the mirror images are so crucial as to clinch the issue between Westernized Krishnan and traditional Kamala. Though she does not criticize her husband for his lack of confidence in the ethic of non-violence, she makes him realize his lapse by her suggestive silence. We notice towards the end of this episode a sense of frustration and failure in Krishnan, as the following passage suggests:

> He wasn't happy but he was more at peace with himself as he looked at the bare walls and up at the high white ceiling, with the suspended fan spinning slowly from it. The *rebellion* had failed. Others had paid for it with their lives, but his own life would flow down the prescribed course unaltered. Indeed, measured by the consequences, there had been no *rebellion.* It was a mirage, an imagined exclamation mark. Undoubtedly Kruger would have called it *Maya.* But the family, the career, the forward look, all that was reality could never be brought to admit it. (51, emphasis added)

The passage is not only interesting but significant, in the sense that it suggests the ambivalence that takes a deep root in Krishnan's mind. The implicit contrast between rebellion, reality, and *Maya* recurs throughout the text with varying degrees of emphasis. The major symbols in the novel—the dance of Siva and the temple—seem to explicate the concepts of rebellion, reality and *Maya*.

The Hindu traditional marriage is not based on the principle of equality of sexes, but is rooted in the idea of acceptance. We may say, once a wife, always a wife. When Krishnan and Kamala shift to New Delhi, because of Krishnan's appointment as an officer in the Central Secretariat, a situation arises which brings "rebellion," "reality," and "*Maya*" into the foreground. Krishnan's relationship with Cynthia and his consequent alienation from Kamala may be analyzed from this point of view. Krishnan's growing fascination for Cynthia may be profitably construed as an act of rebellion against the ruthless hierarchy of the family. The following dialogue between the two drives home the point:

> "Don't worry," she reassured him. "You can be as rude as you like. It just shows how badly your subconscious wants me."
>
> He couldn't help smiling but he had to remind her. "Aren't you forgetting that Kamala is my wife?"
>
> She got to the crux of it with her usual directness. "Why did you marry her?"
>
> "In order to get married."
>
> "If I weren't so perceptive, I would call that an unintelligent answer."
>
> "If you were perceptive, you would realize that it wasn't meant to be intelligent. It was supposed to be adequate." (80)

The above dialogue may suggest that the text spins the hackneyed form of a love-triangle. But what is significant in terms of the total meaning of the text is the contrast between intelligence and adequacy. Krishnan seems to think that the Hindu view of acceptance as the basis of marriage is inadequate. He confirms his views in an oblique way when he tells Cynthia, "Somewhere, somehow my life has got to grow up, it has to live with the problems of my soil and people. Kamala's Indian, intensely so, not simply in what she knows and does, but deep down, in ways that I can only sense and don't even want to understand." (81) It can't be hastily concluded that Krishnan says this either to be fair to his wife or to cajole Cynthia. In this context, we are reminded of the advice the American professor gives to Nalini, which has been cited earlier: Human mind "isn't a sponge, mopping up information. It ought to be a kind of light, shining into the facts and revealing their pattern." Krishnan's frequent observations on Aquinas, Sankara, temples, and Nataraja and the Cosmic Dance indicate that his mind is just a sponge, mopping up information, and not a light that could evaluate and illuminate that information. When he says that "Wherever a Brahmin is there is a temple," it only prsents "the hammer of force and not the mirror of protest." (41) While the hammer signifies what is adequate, the mirror suggests what is intelligent.

The Krishnan-Cynthia relationship, which forms an integral part of Chapter V of the novel, has an appropriate caption, "The Rebellion." We have discussed earlier the significance of rebellion by emphasizing the crucial role of the hammer image. To think that "From accepting the family's decisions he passes on to accepting Cynthia's decisions, which is easy, because she has a stronger will, until Krishnan suddenly realizes the mistake of his choice"[3] is a value judgment that overlooks Krishnan's inherent bent towards rebellion, signified by the hammer image. A careful scrutiny of the text seems to suggest that Krishnan strives to make the spiritual and the sensual worlds extensions of each other. When he looks into the "grave eyes" (166) of the priest in Mutthra temple, he realizes that the kind of extension he wants to achieve has its own shortcomings. When Cynthia's demands on his privacy become more aggressive, he tells her, "You've no right . . . to ask for *a total commitment*. When I lost her I abandoned some of myself. It was much more than I thought. It wasn't simply what I left with her, but so many other loyalties and attachments—to her world, her society and mine too, which just can't be re-created on our *island*." (175, emphasis added).

The phrase "a total commitment" is in perfect accord with Krishnan's intrinsic loyalty to the concept of rebellion. He seems to have an innate aversion to anything that amounts to a total commitment. The island image, on the other hand, seems to convey the idea that he is slowly graduating from the hammer of force to the mirror of protest. The "grave eyes" of the priest is an analogue of the mirror image.

From the foregoing analysis, we may conclude that Krishnan is not able to reconcile himself to the idea of a total commitment. As has been suggested earlier, he is eager to do what is adequate but not what is intellectually satisfactory. A crisis-ridden atmosphere may stimulate one's intelligence, especially of a person who scoffs at commitment. His return to Kamala, who is serving the refugees in Shantihpur, may be interpreted as an intelligent decision prompted by his failure to make the spiritual world an extension of the sensual. He seems to get rid of the notion that a Brahmin's "reasoning processes are extremely complex." (201) His journey to Shantihpur is motivated by the conviction that he would receive a cordial welcome because he is aware of Kamala's total commitment to the values she cherishes. He returns to Kamala not to seek her forgiveness but to see his own image reflected in her eyes. The following passage implicitly suggests that Kamala is the mirror in which Krishnan beholds what he is in himself:

> He let his silence speak to her first, since she was a child of darkness, her quietness spun out of it, her eyes with that softened serenity of the moon emerging into a rain-washed sky. He needed no words to tell her he had come back, and she gave in to his returning, accepting all of him, the hot face, the torn clothes, the blood-crushed bandage, the body he had become, without asking for its history. She did not chide him with any explicit reproof, did not mention, however matter-of-factly, the stark conditions he had forced her into, did not even indulge herself in that sudden accession of happiness which might have made clear how much he had denied her. (206)

The image "the moon emerging into the rain-washed sky" unmistakably suggests that a Brahmin's thought processes are not necessarily complex. It is precisely in this context that the text's central images find a happy integration. The Dark Dancer and the Dance do not lead the self away from the family and society but fuse them with reality at a higher level. On the occasion of Krishnan's marriage with Kamala, a concert is arranged, in which, as a lady sings of Siva dancing in the great temple of Chidambaram, Krishnan's theory of adequacy intervenes to distort the perennial significance of the Cosmic Dance: "He wondered how strong the disciplined surface was, a man's life foreseen with all the precision of ages, stretched taut as the skin which the drummer's fingers caressed, over the energy of the dark, jubilant waters." (29) But when he encounters the image of Nataraja of Chidambaram in Kamala's tent at Shantihpur, the response is different and intelligence-oriented. The symbolic expressivity of Nataraja "was not the catharsis of art—there was no purgation, no refinement, no transmutation of the strength of darkness. It was as if one were raised into the mystery's center, into the transformation of the god's eye, as if the destruction shimmering on the leaping muscles, sucking down the thin wail of the dying man, was not a barbarism to be subdued, a violence to be disciplined, but a jubilation that absorbed the flesh, the rivers and the peaks of comprehension being but one hair of the *unanswered stillness*." (225, emphasis added) The "unanswered stillness," as Krishnan seems to realize after the death of Kamala, is also significatory of the temple. There emerges a clear image of the temple as Krishnan immerses the ashes of Kamala in the Ganges:

> The urn was emptied, the ashes cast out upon the gentle current and the world focused again, the sorrow and the elation, all those whom desire had jostled down the steps, to be healed, to be blessed, to wash away the dead, the weight of error, gathered together in superstition and fear, in charlatanry and the throngs of the truth, in the *temple's* silence and the clanging of carnivals, the deep sincerity mingling with gaudiness, so that each was the condition in which the other found

itself. (289,emphasis added)

The above passage subtly fuses the basic symbols and, at the same time, gives them a metaphysical resonance in which the assertion, "Wherever a Brahmin is, there is a temple," (167) is reversed so as to mean that wherever a temple is, there is a Brahmin. As Swami Chidbhavananda points out, "The temple that the Hindu has conceived and constructed is a replica of the divine possibilities in man."[4] The word "Brahmin" acquires a multiple meaning—one in whom tumult and silence, intelligence and imagination, and commitment and detachment acquire a refined amalgamation. Krishnan's home-coming, his parents's anxiety to see him married to an eligible bride, his marriage with Kamala, his separation from her, his relationship with Cynthia and the breakdown of that relationship, his return to Shantihpur to join Kamala, her re-acceptance, her death, which seems to bring apparent peace to the riot-torn Shantihpur, and his ultimate acceptance of Lord Krishna's message in the *Gita* constitute the plot of the novel. As the plot evolves, the reader notices the social and the metaphysical perspectives by gradually absorbing the symbolic significance of the temple and the dance of Nataraja. Krishnan and Kamala come from a traditional family in which ritual plays an important part. In the Hindu family tradition, ritual is like a bridge to a higher kind of reality. It is the spirit with which rituals are performed that is more important than rituals themselves. But at the same time it cannot be said that rituals by themselves are meaningless. It is here that the image of Nataraja earns that kind of symbolic spread which makes it ubiquitous in the text. Harrex has cogently argued, in his book *The Fire and the Offering*, that *The Dark Dancer* convincingly demonstrates the author's mature understanding and assimilation of the perennial theme of Eliot's *Four Quartets*.[5] No doubt, words like "beginning," "end," "still-point," "stillness," and "center" recur in Rajan's text too often to go unnoticed. It is a critical commonplace of Eliot scholarship that the poet tried to acquire for the self the timeless in time. The thrust of *The Dark Dancer*, on the other hand, seems to forge itself on the theme of action, or what in Hindu thought is known as Karma. This seems to be borne out by the image of Nataraja. Celebrated orientalists like Ananda Coomaraswami have meticulously explicated the metaphysical specificities and the semantics of the image. But one has to take into consideration its meaning and suggestion from the text under review. Siva and Parvathi (Siva and Sakti) constitute what is popularly known as the Cosmic Family. The Dark Dancer—Nataraja—signifies the alteration of joy and terror, which are not fused but which are supposed to co-exist. Kamala's stay in Shantihpur makes her learn the significance of co-existing with joy and terror. Because Shantihpur is torn by the communal riots that came in the wake of the Partition, she realizes the profound meaning of terror in its physical and metaphysical manifestations. She is dedicated and committed to the service of suffering humanity, which brings joy amidst terror. Although she appears to be terrified by the Hindus who pursue the Muslim girl, her sense of dedication and the joy that accompanies it make her stand in their way. The very fact that they stab her to death may be taken as a kind of release from tumult and terror to the realm of joy. Krishnan, who has been a spectator to the disastrous and violent communal broil, feels that "he saw Kamala not simply standing fast but thrusting erectly, passionately, forward, seeming almost to float against the knife. He was shocked by her beauty, her inwardness suddenly stripped bare, the unwavering and almost eerie arrogance, as if for the first time she was meeting her true lover." (273-74) The words "erectly," "passionately," "beauty," "inwardness," "unwavering," and "true lover" seem to authenticate the observations made earlier. This impression is reinforced by the chapter "The Dark Dancer," especially by the following passage:

> She put her hand in his and led him out, swinging his hand with an animation that might have seemed almost childlike if her constant seriousness had not qualified it. But this time her seriousness was different. Her face was not pulled together by the concerns and questions which her reaching out to others must have collected or even by the will to overwhelm despondency. It had relaxed into a serenity, friendly and yet aloof, as if something within her had been settled but as if, also, the happiness that the settlement had brought her had

> already been given to something else. Her lips, finely chiseled, always fastidious, now seemed almost sculptural in their chastity. Her eyes remained lustrous, but under the softness he was aware of a brilliance which was not just the reflection of the starry, enveloping night. She walked with her diminutive shoulders squared a little, as if a strength in her had been touched into life, the circlet of white flowers floating in her hair's blackness, she walked with a blossoming, a queenliness almost of dignity, and there was no question that she was now at peace. (271)

The passage cited above comes just before the final disaster, which takes Kamala's life. The words "childlike," "serenity," "chiseled," "sculptural," "softness," "brilliance," "night," "blackness," "queenliness," and "dignity" energize the passage, giving it almost a dancing rhythm. The childlike quality of Kamala is qualified by her constant seriousness. Her face shows friendliness, yet it remains aloof. The suggestion that "she walked with a blossoming, a queenliness almost of dignity" connects the passage with the idea of the Cosmic Dance. This inference is possible because the image of Nataraja has so many layers of meaning, some of which could be seen in the passage above. Even here the opposites are not fused, they remain as they are. This seems to be a characteristic of most modernist texts, which employ poetic or symbolic language to communicate the co-existence of opposites. Hermann Hesse wrote that "If he were a musician . . . he could without difficulty write a two-part melody in which the two lines of notes and sounds would complement, combat, determine and correspond to each other, which would at every point be mutually and reciprocally related in the most vital and intimate way: and yet any one able to read music would always be able to see and hear each separate note along with its contrary and complementary note, its brother, its enemy, its antipode."[6] *The Dark Dancer* seems to have been organized on the basis of Hermann Hesse's theory. The self is in harmony with and in rebellion against the family, and society is turbulent and peaceful. To put it in another way, from start to finish, Krishnan is attached and detached, participates and withdraws, is hopeful and despondent. Towards the end of the novel, he thinks of the following advice of Lord Krishna to Arjuna:

> He who seeks freedom
> Thrusts fear aside,
> Thrusts aside anger
> And puts off desire:
> Truly that man
> Is made free forever.
> When thus he knows me
> The end, the author
> Of every offering
> And all austerity,
> Lord of the worlds
> And the friends of all men
> O son of Kunti
> Shall he not enter
> The peace of my presence?[7]

He takes the advice "not as a strange meaning, a light in a desolate sky, but as a condition to which his life could work, even through the repetitions and frustrations." (308) The key phrase in this context appears to be "a condition to which his life could work." As has been said earlier, the focus in *The Dark Dancer* appears to be on action. Krishnan's awareness of the significance of action evolves from what is adequate to what is possible, to what is necessary and responsible, and, ultimately, to what appears to be commensurate with the demands of the self, the family and society, as signified by the dance of Nataraja, for which Kamala becomes a symbolic analogue, because her outward and inward self-expression is significatory of what the Dark Dancer is and means, in the sense that there is equilibrium in the midst of oscillation, and harmony behind the seeming discord.

After Kamala's death, Krishnan's parents try to persuade him to marry again. His mother opens the newspaper and casually goes through the column of marriage advertisements. She finds something interesting and reads it aloud to the members present:

> A *Vadama* girl has no objection to a widower. She's a Bachelor of Arts, in public finance and European history. But she sings well and plays the *veena* also." (300)

The above passage is an apt preface to Rajan's second novel, *Too Long in the West*. The two novels in a way converge on the institution of arranged marriage. *The Dark Dancer* brings to the fore some of the perennial issues that haven't found or are likely to find any settlement in a developing traditional country like India. As has been stated earlier, journey to the West or journey to the East may not be interpreted as a confrontation of cultures. The journey is meaningful in that one's sojourn in an alien country may serve the purpose of authenticating not the alien values but the values of the culture to which one is born. This significant idea is given a symphonic orchestration in *The Dark Dancer*. The social and the personal embarrassments of the institution of arranged marriage are dramatized in *Too Long in the West* by employing parody as the organizing principle of the narrative.

Sambasivan, a lecturer by profession, tries to play the role of a benevolent despot in Mudalur, a remote village in South India. He invests most of his savings to create an autonomous and self-sufficient community in the village. He invariably spends his summer vacation there, trying to improve his residence, which he calls Hillview. He has a son and a daughter, Gopal and Nalini. He sends Nalini to Columbia University for her advanced studies, in spite of his wife's strong protests. We are not told in which subject Nalini receives special instruction in Columbia. On the eve of her return from America, he issues the following matrimonial advertisement in *The Hindu:*

> *Vadama* girl, educated yet domesticated. Fair of face, ravishing of form. Unprecedented paragon will marry whoever deserves her. (23)

Even before Nalini arrives at Mudalur, a few bridegrooms who think that they deserve her flock to the place. Satyamurti arrives first, from Kumbakonam, and announces himself to Sambasivan's family as "truth-teller." (28) On her way home, Nalini meets another suitor who calls himself Kalyanasundaram, which means "beautiful marriage." (55) He is a specialist in arranged marriages. His motives are not frivolous. He is engaged in acquiring knowledge about arranged marriages. As he says, his ambition is to acquire "knowledge to fight the arranged marriage, to expose it in all its revolting nakedness, its threats, its bribes and its pitiful desperations. Knowledge with which to destroy this malignant canker which is eating out the heart of Hindu society." (57) The next suitor is Viswakarman. He is a journalist, and says, "I am not simply a reporter but a master of style. In fact I am a master of many styles. When I was a child I wrote like Middleton Murry. I have successfully imitated all the Nobel Prize Winners. I am now maturing from early to late Eliot." (74) The last suitor, Kubera, is engaged in the trade of cosmetics. He tells Nalini, "I knew I was responsible for something in your beauty. From the moment I came into this room I had that faint, unmistakable feeling of achievement. Without Kubera such hair could not exist. With me it can call to every woman from every dressing-table through the length and breadth of India, Pakistan, Ceylon and Madagascar. Not just as a dream, but as a living possibility, a sleek, velvety, glowing loveliness of darkness." (91) The last to join the company of suitors is Ernest, who has come to India as a representative of the World Health Organization, engaged in checking the growth of malaria in India. Nalini knew him in America and feels delighted to see him in India.

Thus we find that the institution of arranged marriage is dramatized in terms of a *swayamvara*, a transitional institution which prevailed in ancient India. In this context one thinks of the *swayamvara* of Draupadi, Damayanti, and a host of other princesses. In the novel under consideration, all the five suitors are interviewed by Nalini. Since the interview is based on the principle of parody, we may suggest that Sambasivan, Nalini's father, plays the role of an ancient king who would give away his daughter to the most deserving of the suitors. But the point that one should not miss is the status of Nalini within the narrative framework. According to the text, she stayed in America for three years. Would it be possible to say that she lived in the West too long? It is here that the ironic foregrounding seems appropriate. On her way home to Mudalur in a bullock-cart,

> she thought of Draupadi and of a splendid young man bending a Gandiva bow. But the thought did not reassure her. She was realistic about her face and didn't expect it to launch a thousand ships; but it would have been flattering to daydream in the Western tradition, to have a valorous knight-errant flaunt her emblem and challenge all to combat on her behalf. Far more flattering certainly than being pawned like poor Draupadi at a dice game, merely to satisfy *a warrior's code of conduct.* (66, emphasis added)

The phrase "a warrior's code of conduct" seems to suggest the ironic placement of the Eastern and the Western traditions of the institutions of courtly love. What saves the situation for Nalini is the passion of Raman, a barber's son, who becomes a rebel, to overthrow the despotism of Sambasivan. When Raman gathers most of the villagers and surrounds Sambasivan's fort (Hillview), a serious situation develops. He accuses the despot and his family of violating the moral purity and the environmental perfection of Mudalur by having liaison with a foreigner. Ernest's jeep and D.D.T become symbols of evil. Kubera's expedition to the mountain on the outskirts of the village to gather the magic mangoes ends in disaster, because of a heavy storm. Exposure to the winds and rain affects the health of Guruswami, one of the participants in the expedition. Raman takes advantage of this and tries to rouse the villagers to attack Sambasivan and his family. The crowd insists, along with Raman, that Nalini should immediately choose her partner in order to vindicate herself. Nalini visits Guruswami and, after saying a few good words, tells him that Mudalur is not a place where things get too serious. What happens here deserves a sensible ending. In fact the sensible ending to her *swayamvara* takes the form of her placing the garland round Raman's neck. While the crowd applauds her decision, Raman loses his temper and threatens Nalini that later she would regret her decision. But she tells him, in what appears to be the most revealing passage, "My dear, deluded, insufferable future husband, as usual you've no idea what you're talking about. You haven't been in the land of the idle rich. But I've been there for three years, living *recklessly* on my poor father's fortune. I've *cooked* more than a thousand meals. I've *stitched* and *laundered* my own clothes. I've scrubbed the floor twice every week. I've put out the *garbage*. I've even *cleaned* the toilet. Have you done any of that with your working-class hands?" (86-87, emphasis added) "Too long in the West" has not in any way contributed to enhance Nalini's sense of the affluent society. Even in the affluent society, somebody has to do the domestic chores like cooking, stitching, scrubbing, and cleaning. What seems to have changed is Nalini's imaginative and mental horizon. Her stay abroad has made her acquire supreme confidence in herself so as to make her say to her mother, "I can look after myself." (79)

As Wayne C. Booth says, "every parody refers at every point to historical knowledge that is in a sense 'outside itself'—that is, previous literary works—and thus to more or less probable genres."[8] While using the idea of a *swayamvara*, a plot device in many ancient and medieval Hindu epics and romances, the narrator doesn't forget that its use as a plot device in a fictional work makes it a parody, thereby giving him a chance to make that fiction an incisive social comment. No doubt, *Too Long in the West* may be taken as a scathing criticism of the institution of arranged marriage. But what is more significant is the subtle ironic suggestion of the title *Too Long in the West*. When Nalini tells Kalyanasundaram that she stayed in America for three years, he says:

> It's far too long. . . . We're independent now. We've different attitudes and different standards. *We're Indians, not mimics of the whiteman.* We've changed and you've changed, but in the wrong direction. You won't fit in. You've joined the lost generation, out of place everywhere and acceptable nowhere. You'll always be *an exile and an alien, a self-created foreigner, a refugee from yourself.* You can't belong. You'll live in two worlds and fall between two stools. (55, emphasis added)

The above passage acts as a thematic link between the two novels we have just discussed. In terms of the Indian social landscape, the re-entry of an Indian who has stayed too long in the West may not be an alienation or loss of one's traditional moorings. Krishnan and Nalini, in spite of the ordeals they face, seem to retain what they have inherited. They are members of Hindu society, and their journey to the West and their return to the East do signify the inviolability of the self that has its roots in the social and the familial milieus that have become part and parcel of themselves.

NOTES

1. Balachandra Rajan, *Too Long in the West* (Bombay: Jaico, 1961), p. 48.
2. Balachandra Rajan, *The Dark Dancer* (New Delhi: Arnold-Heinemann, 1976), p. 167.
3. Meenakshi Mukherjee, *The Twice-Born Fiction: Themes and Techniques of the Indian Novel in English,* 2nd ed., (New Delhi: Arnold-Heinemann (India), 1974), p. 85.
4. Swami Chidbhavananda, *Facets of Brahman Or The Hindu God* (Tirupparaitturai: Sri Ramakrishna Tapovanam, 1971), p. 123.
5. S.C. Harrex, "Dancing in the Dark: Balachandra Rajan and T.S. Eliot," *The Fire and the Offering: The English-Language Novel of India 1935-1970* (Calcutta: Writers Workshop, 1977), I, pp. 185-195.
6. James McFarlane, "The Mind of Modernism," in *Modernism*: 1890-1930, ed. Malcolm Bradbury and James McFarlane, pp. 88-89.
7. *The Dark Dançer*, p. 308. Quoted from *The Song of God: Bhagavad-Gita*, trans. Swami Prabhavananda and Christopher Isherwood (New York: The American Library, 1954), p. 62.
8. Wayne C. Booth, *A Rhetoric of Irony* (Chicago: The University of Chicago Press, 1974), p. 123.

Raja Rao and the Imperial Self

Krishnan, the protagonist of *The Dark Dancer*, says that "Wherever a Brahmin is, there is a temple."[1] Krishnan is so self-conscious that he cannot unburden himself of his "Brahminhood." Ramaswamy, the protagonist of *The Serpent and the Rope*, appears to be more self-conscious than Krishnan. He begins his narration with a self-conscious assertion that "I was born a Brahmin—that is, devoted to Truth and all that. 'Brahmin is he who knows Brahman,' etc., etc."[2] Towards the end of the narrative, he tells Catherine that "A Brahmin is he who knows Brahman," and hastens to add that "There is another, a roguish definition. A Brahmin is he who loves a good banquet." (406) Govinda Nair in *The Cat and Shakespeare* recites to his friend Ramakrishna Pai the *Astavakra Samhita*, and tells him:

> I have done a good job. I have explained to the Brahmin what Brahman is. Brahmin is he who knows Brahman, etc., etc. Ruling princes taught *sadhus* the Truth in the Upanishadic times. Now Nairs alone can teach the Truth in the world.[3]

The above passage, if placed in the context of Raja Rao's seminal themes in the entire corpus of his writing, exemplify the ironic perspective from which his texts are organized. Ramaswamy in *The Serpent and the Rope* talks about everything under the sun. He reflects on space, time and eternity, and illusion and reality, and ultimately announces his humble intention to seek the feet of his Guru in Travancore. The text doesn't say whether the Guru is a Brahmin or a Nair. But his second definition of a Brahmin as "he who loves a good banquet" perhaps suggests the kind of self-consciousness which makes one aware of one's own limitations.

Raja Rao's four novels to-date—*Kanthapura, The Serpent and the Rope, The Cat and Shakespeare*, and *Comrade Kirillov*—dramatize the ways and means through which his protagonists evolve to that stage of awareness which consists in knowing and evaluating their limitations. It also consists in unburdening themselves of the awful superiority and prestige associated with a Brahmin in a caste-ridden society. For example, what is significant in *Kanthapura* is not the electrifying effect of the Gandhian ethic on a rural community but the transformation it brings in in Moorthy, who comes from a higher caste.

Raja Rao has received extensive and varied critical attention in India and abroad. His narrative and linguistic innovations and his varied interests in philosophy, aesthetics, sociology, and politics have been explored and explicated. C.D. Narasimhaiah and M.K. Naik have written excellent monographs, which elucidate the complexities of the entire *oeuvre*. But the more relevant aspect in discussing a writer like Raja Rao seems to be the images of society that are foreground in his texts. The following pages analyze the texts so as to bring out their aesthetic and contextual relevance in terms of their socio-cultural implications. For the sake of clarity of the argument, the most convenient point of entry into the fictional corpus of Raja Rao is *The Cat and Shakespeare*. Raja Rao calls it "A Tale of Modern India." One may doubt whether the Trivandrum of 1940s can be taken as an image of modern India. The nature of Raja Rao's achievement and its relevance to us largely depend on the means and the method we employ in answering the question posed earlier. The centre of the plot in *The Cat and Shakespeare* is Ration Office No. 66, in which Govindan Nair is a clerk. He and the narrator, Ramakrishna Pai, who works in the Revenue Office, are neighbours. A long dilapidated wall divides the neighbours. Ramakrishna Pai, who is transferred from Pattanur to Trivandrum, is compelled to stay away from his wife and children. He finds in Govindan Nair a warm host and a generous friend, and in Shantha, a woman who wants him. We see the Nair through the eyes of a Brahmin, a Brahmin who is conscious of his caste. The Ration Office brings together characters who belong to various castes and communities. Bhoothalinga Iyer, the boss, is a Brahmin. John,

Abraham, Syed Sahib, and Ramakrishna Pai are Govindan Nair's colleagues. The narrator confesses that Govindan Nair knows Sanskrit and has read the basic texts on Hinduism and Hindu philosophy, of which, though a Brahmin, he himself is absolutely ignorant. The Ration Office and the people who run it may be taken as India in miniature. The British had the justification of organizing ration shops to achieve equitable distribution of food stuffs: they were financing a war against tyranny. What justification can one advance for continuing the British institution of rationing—with ration offices, ration shops, and ration cards—so many years after the British left India? Most people who work in the Ration Office build houses and acquire wealth and influence. John, for example, builds a house. As Govindan Nair remarks humorously, "He built a house, that is John did. He built a modest little house. He said it was done from the proceeds of his wife's property's sale. Her grandmother had just died. Everybody has a grandmother, you know." (27) This indicates that exploitation and corruption always exist and make some people rich and some people poor. Frequently, bags of rice suddenly disappear; sometimes, they go unaccounted. A lot of faking goes on in the issue of ration cards. False statistics are conveniently used and numbers are manipulated, so that owners of hotels thrive while the man in the street goes without food. Govindan Nair is aware of what happens in the Ration Office. For example, he says, "Rats eat up accounts. That is how we explained away the ration given to Kolliathur village. When the big boss asked, 'Where are the files?' we made such a grand search. First my boss said: 'We have misplaced it.' Then he said: 'We do not think we have it in this office.' Finally he wrote: 'Eaten away by rats. Please ask the Public Works Department Officer to come to Ration Office No. 66 for inspection. Two reports on rat pest remain unanswered.'" (27) The passage may be construed as a fine satire on the way in which most government departments function in India. But the point that has to be emphasized is that Govindan Nair's knowledge of the corrupt practices of his colleagues doesn't make him a cynic. In other words, it doesn't in any way affect his warmth and goodwill towards his colleagues. His attitude towards human weakness and frailty is more charitable than his attitude towards corruption. In order to fulfil an obligation of his boss to a woman with whom he (the boss) had a clandestine relationship, Govindan Nair courts arrest and is imprisoned. Bhoothalinga Iyer, his boss, places a rupee in the treasure pitcher of the sanctorium every time he commits a sin. In order to avoid any fuss about his activities, he tells his wife that the treasure pitcher contains money that would one day help him go to Benares. He requests Govindan Nair to go to Mutthalinga Nayak Street and give the treasure pitcher to a widow called Minakshamma. This is twisted as evidence against Govindan Nair that he took a bribe from a widow whose son owns a ration shop. He seems to have a marvellous sobriety that stands him in good stead in negotiating with all inconceivable situations. M.K. Naik thinks that "Though *The Cat and Shakespeare* can be enjoyed simply as a comic extravaganza and a realistic tale, it is, at the same time, a very ambitious exercise in metaphysical speculation."[4] It may not be easy to unravel the significance of the author's "ambitious exercise in metaphysical speculation." But it is possible to explicate the semantic structure of the tale by invoking the Lawrentian dictum, "Let me hear what the novel says."[5] Govindan Nair himself is a good guide—better than any commentator—in showing the path that leads to an innate confidence in the self. He tells the judge, "Your Lordship, I speak only the truth. If the world of man does not conform to truth, should truth suffer for that reason? If only you knew how I pray every night and say: 'Mother, keep me at the lotus feet of Truth.' The judge can give a judgment. The Government Advocate can accuse. Police Inspector Rama Iyer can muster evidence. But the accused alone knows the truth." (103) In the passage just cited, the word "truth" is so emphasized that the speaker may be misconstrued as one who protests but is not interested in practising what he says. It is precisely here that the comic sense of life and humour come to the rescue of Govindan Nair. Of the many instances that are available in Shakespeare's plays, there is an apt instance in *Much Ado About Nothing*, in which Hero's innocence and chastity are vindicated and her betrothal to Claudio is saved from certain ruin by the innocuous and unpremeditated act of Dogberry and Verges. After arresting Don John's men, Borachio and Conrade, and bringing them to Don

Pedro, Dogberry says, "Marry, sir . . . they have spoken untruths; secondarily, they are slanders; sixth and lastly, they have belied a lady; thirdly, they have verified unjust things; and, to conclude, they are lying knaves."[6] The cat that John presents to Govindan Nair to mock him saves him by making the court clerk trace the paper in which Bhoothalinga Iyer's signature is clearly visible. As the narrator comments:

> It was all due to Govindan Nair. He had, while in prison, written out a whole story to himself. Bhoothalinga Iyer had signed the paper. It had nothing to do with ration permits. It had to do with Bhoothalinga Iyer's extramarital propensities. In this business he came across virtue. So instead of going to Benares he gave the money to the widow of a Brahmin, an Iyengar woman in fact. (The breasts and other things were added to make the story comply with film stories.) The story came true as he wrote it. He was sure that it was a fact. He told himself again and again and told it in court again and again. At night the prison wardens were surprised to see him talking to himself. Actually he thought he was addressing the court. He even made and remade the necessary gestures. Wardens could think he was practising acting. He recited his prose precisely till he knew every situation by heart. That is why he was so cocksure in open court. After all, only a good story that you write yourself from nowhere can be prefect. You can do with it what you want to do with it. (Abraham wrote romantic poetry and he said it did with him what it wanted. So, eventually, he married Myriam, etc.) But Govindan Nair had the liberty the judge did not have. Only the Government Advocate knew everything. A fact is a prisoner. You are free, or you become the prisoner, and the fact is free, etc., etc. So the Government Advocate knew the accused was no accused. He was one with the accused. That showed why the cat went to the Government Advocate first. The cat also kissed the clerk on the neck. (107-8)

This crucial passage demonstrates Govindan Nair's implicit

confidence in the self. The key sentence in the passage appears to be "In this business he came across virtue." Virtue consists in helping people who are in need, not in going to Benares to expiate one's sins. Perhaps it is this conviction that propels him to write about the entire mess in which he is involved. In writing the story, Nair seems to detach himself from the fact that he is subordinate to his boss and focus his imagination on the method of dramatizing it in the court: "He even made and remade the necessary gestures." The total import of the passage is suggested by the narrator's mature reflection that "only a story that you write yourself from nowhere can be perfect." Moreover, the passage juxtaposes fact, fiction, and truth. Truth is not something that is there to be seized and exhibited. What is a fact may appear as a fiction. For example, Bhoothalinga Iyer's sudden death caused by the cat landing on his head may appear as a fiction, just as an elderly advocate in the court considers his relationship with the Brahmin widow "sheer pornography." (101) But the point to be noted in the context of the text is that fictions are not truths but they bring home to men's bosoms and business truths which the self always confirms and authenticates.

From the foregoing analysis, it may be possible to interpret the two major symbols in the text, the cat and Shakespeare. These two symbols are reinforced by another symbol, the house that the narrator dreams of building. A careful perusal of the text suggests that the word "mystery" is associated with Shakespeare. Govindan Nair tells John: "Shakespeare knew every mystery of the ration shop." (63) Just before he makes this statement, Govindan Nair draws a comparison between the Kingdom of Denmark and the Ration Office, making us remember the words of Marcellus to Horatio: "Something is rotten in the state of Denmark."[7] What Govindan Nair seems to suggest is not a parallel between *Hamlet* and what goes on inside the Ration Office but that in Shakespearian imagination everything is possible. As Theseus says in *A Midsummer-Night's Dream,*

> The Poet's eye, in a fine frenzy rolling,
> Doth glance from heaven to earth, from earth to heaven;
> And as imagination bodies forth

> The forms of things unknown, the poet's pen
> Turns them to shapes, and gives to airy nothing
> A local habitation and a name.
> Such tricks hath strong imagination.
> That, if it would but apprehend some joy,
> It comprehends some bringer of that joy;
> Or in the night, imagining some fear,
> How easy is a bush suppos'd a bear?[8]

Govindan Nair has fertile imagination and a refined sense for language, so that he cannot only parody a Shakespearian passage but can eloquently talk about the cat in the cage in Malayalam, Sanskrit, Latin, and English. Imagination and empathy made Shakespeare everything and nothing. Jorge Luis Borges, in a brilliant sketch entitled "Everything and Nothing," makes the following comment:

> History adds that before or after dying he found himself in the presence of God and told him: "I who have been so many men in vain want to be one and myself." The voice of the Lord answered from a whirlwind: "Neither am I any one; I have dreamt the world as you dreamt your work, my Shakespeare, and among the forms in my dream are you, who like myself are many and no one."[9]

The Borgesian text reinforces the idea that poetic imagination and divine imagination are not two different things; in a way, they are one. When an interlocutor asked Raja Rao, "What is the justifications of the name of Shakespeare in the title of *The Cat and Shakespeare?*" Raja Rao said, "Because of the fact that Shakespeare is a sage."[10] A sage is one whose doors of perception are open and refined, so that he can behold the forms of things unknown. Govindan Nair seems to have developed his imagination and sensibility to such a refined degree that he can see the mystery associated with existence in its natural and supernatural dimensions. His message that one ought to trust the mother cat like a kitten may appear cryptic at the human level, but is definitely profound at the divine level. A kitten has implicit faith in the mother cat when it shifts the kitten from place to place. The relationship between the mother cat and the kitten may also be interpreted from the point of view of the Advaita, Visishtadvaita and Dvaita tenets in Indian philosophy, which we shall elaborately discuss with reference to *The Serpent and the Rope*. But here, it can only be pointed out that when we say that existence is a mystery, we are only saying that however much one tries to squeeze the meaning of existence, something or the other would remain unaccounted for and unexplained.

The narrator of the tale, Ramakrishan Pai, always thinks of building a house. Govindan Nair encourages him, because in the traditional view of Hindu society a man who builds his own house is a man of achievement. This traditional view of life, though it gives more importance to the spiritual aspect of human life, does not ignore its material aspect. If one worships Lord Siva by offering *bilva* leaves to the deity, it is assumed that one's material and spiritual needs are taken care of. Even if the deity is propitiated unconsciously, just as a hunter hiding in ambush to shoot a deer or a porcupine made the *bilva* leaves fall on the image of Siva which was there, the consequences will be similar. As the narrator reflects, "It's not the way you worship that is important but what you adore. Even an accidental fall of leaves on Shiva's head got the wicked hunter his vision. And thus the stump of a tree became sacred—and its trefoil sacred, for all that is sacred to God. So when I look from my window eastward, just by the garden wall, I see the stump of a *bilva* tree, thorns visible in the morning sun. And I wonder if God will ever bless me, just like that." (9) Perhaps his association with Govindan Nair has impregnated the mind of the narrator in such a way that his constant prayer is: "Lord, let me build the house." (18) His prayer is answered in the form of Shantha, with whose money he buys the house in which he has been staying. His promotion and prosperity seem to be the blessing for which he has been praying, so that he finally considers that "Truth is such a beautiful thing—a beautiful woman like Shantha loves to hear the truth talked, because it explains her beauty and takes away her responsibility." (115) This metaphysical truth is elaborated by making use of the image of stairs, as in the following passage:

> So that day I walked behind the cat. It went down into the kitchen of the White House and left the litter in the corner of the granary room. Then it went up a series of stone steps. Up and up it went, up the staircase. Everybody bowed as if awed. Then I, too, followed it. This time I would not be defeated. I must win, I said. The winning was easy, for I heard a very lovely music. I was breathless. The staircase suddenly turned, and in went the cat. I stood there white as marble. I looked in and saw everything.
>
> I saw nose (not the nose) and eyes seeing eyes seeing, I saw ears curved to make sound visible, and face and limbs rising in perfection of perfection, for form was it. I saw love yet knew not its name but heard it as sound, I saw truth not as fact but as ignition. I could walk into fire and be cool, I could sing and be silent, I could hold myself and yet not be there. I saw feet. They made flowers on stems and the curved hands of children. I smelled a breath that was of nowhere but rising in my nostrils sank back into me, and found death was at my door. I woke up and found death had passed by, telling me I had no business to be there. Then where was I? Death said it had died. I had killed death. When you see death as death, you kill it. When you say, I am so and so, and you say, I am such and such, you have killed yourself. I remain over, having killed myself. (115-16)

The passage under critical focus defies analysis and explication. The vision that Ramakrishna Pai earns for himself dissolves all dualities. Not only does it dissolve all dualities, it also dissolves ego-consciousness. Death is meaningful only in terms of the ego. To the naked vision death appears only as the collapse of the body and the annihilation of the body-consciousness. When one kills oneself, it only means that one has made a leap, a leap into the forms unknown. This inference is something that one can draw solely with reference to the text under review. If, as Raja Rao puts it, "writing as a *sadhana*,"[11] which means a mode of prayer, *The Cat and*

Shakespeare is a tale that dramatizes the efficacy of training oneself to achieve the kind of anonymity Borges notices in Shakespearean imagination and, at the same time, establish and nourish one's roots in the traditional social forms, which authenticate and vitalize the image of God in man and the image of man in God. Ramaswamy's discursive attempts at and non-discursive modes of apprehending reality constitute a *sadhana* which doesn't achieve any kind of ultimate spiritual fruition but suggests ways and means of achieving it. In *The Serpent and the Rope*, there are innumerable passages which are discursive, in the sense that they make a point which has a metaphysical connotation rather than a psychic suggestion. For example, the following passage:

> Destiny is, I think, nothing but a series of psychic knots that we tie with our own fears. The stars are but efforts made indeterminate. To act, then, is to be proscribed to yourself. Freedom is to leave nothing of yourself outside. The whole of event is the eye of life, and eternity the "I". Never can you escape eternity, for never can you escape that "I". Even when you say you can, it is the "I" saying it. Can the "I" say anything? No, it cannot, no more than eternity can be seen in time. But time seeing itself is eternity, just as wave seeing itself is water. Meanwhile the winds lift and the monsoon blows, and white flakes of wavelets curve and rise, dash and demonstrate, and from crest to crest they cavalcade processioning to the shore. Not wavelet or crest, however breathless with foam is life: water is the meaning of life, or rather the meaning of life is *lila*, play.
>
> Not achievement but self-recognition is pure significance. The extrovert confederates of action must stop, then we leap back to our own safety, our own despiration. The knots are thus undone, and calm as the Mediterranean is the effortless sea.
>
> For the going inward is the true birth. He indeed the Brahmin who turns the crest inward; even if you are a pandit great as Jagannatha Bhatta or learned in logic as Kapila-Charya, the true life, the true Brahminhood commences when

you recognize yourself in your eternity. At some moment you must stop life and look into it. Marriage or maternity, pain or the intimacy of success—love—may dip you into yourself. And as you go on dipping and rising in your inner Ganges murmuring,

> *"Kashi Kshetram Shariram*
> *Tribhuvana jananim vayapim gyana Ganga"*
> "My body, the holy site, is Benares,
> Spreading within me as knowledge, the Ganges,
> Mother of the three worlds."

you undo your knots. It is thus Benares is sacred, and Mother Ganga the absolver of sins. Sin is to think that in acting you are the actor: freedom, that you never could be the doer or enjoyer of an act. In the Ganges of such a life destiny dissolves—and you sail down to your own ocean. (215-16)

The passage makes one think that it is a prose poem. But on re-reading it, we find that the wave and sea imagery is more rhetorical than poetic. The passage in a way suggests the differences between self-introversion and self-extroversion. The "I" in the context of the entire text refers to the transcendent subject. But this transcendental subject becomes the object when the eye turns inward. The cryptic image "time seeing itself in eternity, just as wave seeing itself is water: signifies the perennnial act of seeing, which helps one recognize oneself in one's eternity. In all social activity and intellectual perception, the self dips into itself. The Ganges murmurs that the body itself is Benares and the Ganges flows inside it, spreading knowledge. Knowledge consists in attaining freedom. Freedom consists in getting over the illusion that you are the doer or enjoyer of an act. On the other hand, it is a sin to think that in acting you are the actor. Bondage or freedom "in marriage or maternity, pain or the intimacy of success—love" is eternally intransitive, in the sense that it suggests a state of mind which is discursive and dualistic. Destiny as "a series of psychic knots that we tie with our own fears" suggests a state of bondage. The Ganges in the sense of knowledge can dissolve all fears, in other words, contradiction and duality. Whatever one does dips one into the self. There alone action, social or intellectual, becomes meaningful. It appears as though the self has the kind of perfection which is absolute and incontrovertible. One may, borrowing a phrase from Quentin Anderson, call the self "the imperial self." The text under review and the speaker's tone suggest a non-dualistic view of the self and reality, Advaita, the corner-stone of the *Bhagavad Gita*. As Swami Chidbhavananda says, "Advaita literally means non-dualism. What are termed Jagat and Jiva and Brahman are not really separate entities. Reality is one without a second. It is Existence-Knowledge-Bliss Infinite. It has intrinsic power to manifest Itself as the Jagat and the Jiva. This inherent power is called Maya. Brahman and *Maya* are inseparable. This is the implication of the word Advaita. It is because of his ignorance that the Jiva fancies that he is separate from the universe and the Substratum behind it. With a dawn of knowledge this feeling of difference vanishes. The Reality alone exists. Because of Its *Mayasakti*, It manifests Itself as the Jiva and the Jagat. Resolving this *sakti* into Itself, It also remains unmanifest. In Its kinetic state it is Saguna Brahman (Conditioned Reality), in the static Nirguna (Absolute Reality). As the wave subsides into the ocean the individual soul dissolves into the Absolute. This is emancipation according to the Advaita system of philosophy."[12] The text under review also makes use of the images of the wave and the sea. When the wave subsides into the ocean, there is no sound or friction. Everything is calm as the Mediterranean. What is noticeable here is the secularization of the scripture. Ramaswamy tries to interpret the sacred in a secular context, that is, in terms of his relationship with his wife, Madeleine, and Savithri (family), and his commitment to India (society).

If we look at the mode of narration employed in *The Serpent and the Rope*, we may gain a perspective that would help us in clarifying a number of knotty problems it presents. The narrative presents the consciousness of a single character who also happens to be the protagonist, Ramaswamy. This can be called self-narration, which Proust employs in *A la Recherche du temps perdu* (*Remembrance of the Things Past*). This mode of narration, that is, self-narration, has certain creative possibilities and, at the same time, certain limitations. As Dorrit Cohn cogently remarks, "Contrary to what one might have expected . . . the first-person narrator has less free access to his own past psyche than the omniscient narrator of third-person fiction has to the psyches of his characters. His retrospection depends on a fundamentally different optics: there is no magic mirror corresponding to the magic lens, only the "telescope levelled at time" of which Proust speaks, and by which he means a "real" psychological vision conditioned by memory. This frequently prompts a first-person narrator to mention the plausibility of his cognition, particularly when it involves *the most inchoate moments of his past.*" (Emphasis added)[13] In *The Serpent and the Rope*, Ramaswamy narrates his own story and, while narrating, collapses the chronology in order to give an inclusive vision. But when he claims himself to be a historian, he is not very certain of what he is doing. The novel is not divided into chapters or sections, which suggests that it is a continuous flow, now and then interrupted by innumerable discursive comments on every form of social and spiritual activity. The following passage very well illustrates the significance of the foregoing comments:

> The rest of the story is easily told. In a classical novel it might have ended in palace and palanquin and howdah, or in the high Himalayas, but I am not telling a story here, I am writing the sad and uneven chronicle of a life, my life, with no art or decoration, but with the "objectivity," the discipline of the "historical sciences," for by taste and tradition I am only an historian. (231)

The above passage exemplifies the truth of Raja Rao's own remarks on the aesthetic of *The Serpent and the Rope*. He tells an interlocutor: "The aesthetic is that, sometimes, I like to write like a *Purana*. I like the *Puranic* conception. That is the only conception of novel for me. I don't want to compare my novel with any foreign novel. I don't like to write like a foreign novelist. I am very much Indian and the Indian form is the *Puranic* form. Form comes naturally to me. Hence, it is wrong to study my novels in the light of the Western conception of a well-made novel.''[14]

The author's direction, suggesting the method a reader should adopt in discussing his texts, may not be acceptable to a thorough-going formalist who swears by the intentional fallacy. In considering a text, one has to go beyond formalism, if it helps in unravelling the intricacies of the text. In Sanskrit sacred literature, there are eighteen *Puranas (Ashtadasa Purana).* The authorship of these *Puranas* is attributed to the sage Vyasa, the author of the *Mahabharata.* Most of the *Puranas* have socio-cultural significance, in the sense that they convey a message concerning the way the self should seek *dharma, artha, kama* and *moksha. Moksha* is the ultimate end, the integration of the self and reality, which would dissolve *maya.* A *Purana* contains not one story but a number of stories loosely connected by the purposive narration that conveys a message. It conforms to the Horatian pattern of art providing, at one and the same time, profit and delight. In other words, they exemplify an aesthetic which Abrams called pragmatic. Most *Puranic* stories have a happy blend of realism and fantasy, so that we see in them a fusion of the Barthesian codes and the incomparable metaphysical and philosophical insights. While the first-person narration helps Ramaswamy keep his narration episodic and discursive, his constant preoccupation with the sources of illumination helps him make the narration run like the flow of the Ganges. The various characters that appear and disappear in the narrative contribute a great deal not only in creating diversity but in explicating the meaning and the significance of that diversity, which is a characteristic of *Puranic* narration. There are five significant women characters in the text, whose relationship with the narrator provides a consciousness which is expanding and which, at the same time, differentiates the socio-cultural milieus of the characters themselves. The image of his stepmother, humorously christened Little Mother, with her infant son, Sridhara, on her lap, makes the narrator think of his French wife, Madeleine. He reflects on the various motives which might have propelled her to marry him, and says, ''What I think Madeleine really cared for was a disinterested devotion to any cause, and she loved me partly because she felt India had been wronged by the British, and because she would, in marrying me, know and identify herself with a great people." (18) Whether he loved Madeleine or not, the word "love" seems to earn a multiple meaning:

> To me difference was inborn—like my being the eldest son of my father, or like my grandfather being the Eight-Pillared House Ramakrishnayya, and you had just to mention his name anywhere in Mysore State, even to the Maharaja, and you were offered a seat, a wash, and a meal, and a coconut-and-shawl adieu. To me difference was self-created, and so I accepted that Madeleine was different. That is why I loved her so. In fact, even Little Mother, who sat in front of me—how could I not love her, though she was so different from my own mother? In difference there is the acceptance of one's self as a reality—and the perspective gives the space for love. (19-20)

The above passage enlarges the meaning of love, which makes it possible for the narrator to differentiate between one character and the other and, at the same time, discover a network of relations that makes the difference, paradoxically, a kind of resemblance, as the following unmistakably suggests:

> In some ways—I thought that day, as the boat, now that evening was soon going to fall, was moving upstream, with a fine, clear wind sailing against us—in some ways how like Madeleine was Little Mother. They both had the same shy presence, both rather silent and remembering everything; they loved, too, more than is customary. Both knew by birth that life is no song but a brave suffering, and that at best there are moments of bridal joy with occasionally a drive over a bridge—and then the return to the earth and maybe to widowhood. (20)

When he meets Savithri on his way back from Benares, he feels, "Her presence never said anything, but her absence spoke. Even when she went to speak on the telephone one felt she had a rich, natural grace, and one longed for her to be back. I felt I did not like her, she was too modern for me; she had already started smoking." (31) The phrase "one longed for her to be back" suggests the first impression, which immediately gets itself corrected. He doesn't like the girl because she is too modern when compared to Little Mother. When he meets Savithri again in Paris, he tries again to analyze the difference and the similarity between Savithri and the other women he met, in order to specify what Savithri means to him. That Savithri has a mind that is always absorbed, serious, and sad, but capable of seeing the truth in all its radiance and majesty is the inference he draws from his intimate contact with her. The following seems to affirm this inference:

> For her, I could see, everything was gesture and symbol, and time had been abolished, that the river might run through the night, the tree rise high, the mountains move as on themselves; that words be spoken as though left behind, and the body itself be a casket in which one sees oneself, not as limb and form, but as light cooled into space, as a gift, an object, a truth. All was secret to her but herself—so all was a legend, and every event a wonder. (126)

When he meets her again, in London, she performs a simple ceremony of devotion. She kneels and places her head on his feet. On that occasion he offers her the toe-rings given by Little Mother as a gift to Madeleine, her daughter-in-law. This symbolic act creates another meaning for love, it is "like a sacred text, a cryptogram, with different meanings at different hierarchies of awareness." (213) When he thinks of his sister, Saroja, the perspective doesn't alter. When he beholds her at the age of seventeen, he wonders and feels that she "would never say anything important to any one, and yet by some abrupt inconsequentiality she would say something you had been waiting to name." (49)

From the foregoing analysis, a significant point emerges. In Hindu society, women have a significant place. It is not a question of equality of rights and privileges between men and women but a question of the place of women in the awareness of the self, in the network of familial relations and in the social organization as a whole. The following passage amply illustrates the point:

> Woman is the earth, air, ether, sound; woman is the microcosm of the mind, the articulations of space, the knowing in knowledge; the woman is fire, movement clear and rapid as the mountain stream; the woman is that which seeks against that which is sought. To Mitra she is Varuna, to Indra she is Agni, to Rama she is Sita, to Krishna she is Radha. Woman is the meaning of the word, the breath, touch, act; woman, that which reminds man of which he is and reminds herself through him of that which she is. Woman is kingdom, solitude, time; woman is growth, the gods, inherence; the woman is death, for it is through woman that one is born; woman rules, for it is she, the universe. (352)

In Hindu mythology, which is largely drawn from the *Puranas*, there is a cult of worship associated with the Mother, the consort of Lord Siva. This is specifically indicated in one of the *Puranas* called *Sri Devepurana.* (This has been elaborately discussed in the chapter on Rajan.) Sankara, the celebrated theorist of Advaita, has written a number of hymns on the Divine Mother, which the narrator quotes often. It appears as though absolute reality can be envisioned and known either as the Father or as the Mother. All virility and fecundity, and peace and joy that the sacred texts enunciate is based on the principle of unity in diversity, just as India itself could be comprehended only in terms of unity in diversity. The narrator seems to have considered the philosophical cruxes in the Hindu vision of life and arrived at the following metaphysical formulation which, as we have noted earlier, secularizes the scripture:

> The world is either unreal or real—the serpent or the rope. There is no in-between-the-two—and all that's in-between is poetry, is sainthood. You might go on saying all the time, "No, no, it's the rope," and stand in the serpent. And looking at the rope from the serpent is to see paradises, saints,

> avataras, gods, heroes, universes. For wheresoever you go, you see only with the serpent's eyes. Whether you call it duality or modified duality, you invent a belvedere to heaven, you look at the rope from the posture of the serpent, you feel you are the serpent—you are—the rope is. But in true fact, with whatever eyes you see there is no serpent, there never was a serpent. You gave your own eyes to the falling evening and cried, "Ayyo! Oh! It's the serpent!" You run and roll and lament, and have compassion for fear of pain, others', or your own. You see the serpent and in fear you feel you are it, the serpent, the saint. One—the Guru—brings you the lantern; the road is seen, the long, white road, going with the statutory stars. "It's only the rope." He shows it to you. And you touch your eyes and *know* there never was a serpent. Where was it, where, I ask you? The poet who saw the rope as serpent became the serpent, and so a saint. Now, the saint is shown that his sainthood was identification, not realization. The actual, the real has no name. The rope is no rope to itself. (335)

If we juxtapose the above metaphysical formulation with what Ramaswamy writes in the tenth chapter of his thesis, we can see a sort of consistency in the narrative focus and the thematic alignment in the text. Ramaswamy writes:

> My tenth chapter was especially difficult because it was going to deal with the metaphysical symbolism of paradise. According to the Hindu concept there is not only *satya* and *asatya*, Truth and untruth, but also *mitya*, illusion—like the horns on the head of a rabbit, or the son of a barren woman. Paradise, I argued, was the inversion of Truth. To see frankly is not necessarily to see fairly—you can look at a thing upside down. After all the deer went to drink water at the mirage. The Impossible becomes the beautiful. (377)

A close look at the metaphysical vocabulary of the above two passages suggests to us the narrative constraints and the limits of logic when the narrator-protagonist tries to describe the ineffable.

In the first passage, the world is either unreal or real, the serpent or the rope. Ramaswamy doesn't conceive of any middle term. In the second passage, there are three concepts: truth, untruth, and illusion. The serpent is associated, in the first passage, with Paradise, saints, *avataras*, gods, heroes, and universes. Moreover, the serpent is something that creates a sense of fear. The Guru alone, with his knowledge (lantern), can show to the disciple that there never was any serpent. It is just a rope. As Shyamala A. Narayan points out, "The key concept of Sankara's advaita is *maya*, the in-between-the-two which Ramaswamy disowns. Sankaracharya did not consider the world unreal—he postulated three kinds of being: the real (*sat*), the unreal (*asat*), and *maya* or *mithya* (illusion). Sankara considered the world the realm of *maya*, something which defies strict classification into real or unreal *(sad-asad-vilaksana)*."[15] Ramaswamy's deviations from Sankara's Advaita need not detain us here; what is interesting from our point of view is the way in which Ramaswamy uses the metaphysical idiom to enlarge the narrative context. The first passage occurs when he and Madeleine are sorting out their differences. When she asks him, "What is it separates us, Rama?" he tells her, "India." (331) Making a brave attempt to convince her, he tells her, "Love is not a feeling; it is, you might say, a stateless state, the whole condition of oneself." (331) In order to emphasize the significance of the Vedanta in terms of the Hindu view of life as against the Buddhist view, with which Madeleine tries to entangle him once again in the familial groove, Ramaswamy expounds the-serpent-and-the-rope problematic. But what appears to be uppermost in his mind is the master-idea of the Guru. In the second passage we have earlier considered, we find him intellectualizing and shaping the problem at hand, the Albigensian heresy. The first passage has a rhetorical flourish, and the second passage, intellectual rigour. When we look at the narrative as a whole, it appears that the-serpent-and-the-rope problematic doesn't in any way mitigate the suffering, the pain, the dislocation of human relationships, the social encumbrances, and the intellectual embarrassments the protagonist tries to organize within the framework of his narration. For example, he resorts to the use of a diary, which has some significance in the organization of the text. The following excerpt from a note in his diary amply demonstrates the tension that exists between him and Madeleine after the loss of their first child:

> A woman hates a male when he withdraws. She cannot accept his defeat—his defeat is the defeat of her womanhood. She must be the juice of his love, she must give him again and again that which he asks for, till his asking itself becomes a disgust. Then the woman has contempt for him, she rubs her breast on his back, she whispers sweet things to his ears, her body speaks where no words could speak, and she lifts him up and takes him into herself, like a mother a child. Then you want to take a cactus branch and beat her and scratch her all over. You want to bite her lip and pull the breast away from her chest, and taste the good blood of her wounds. You want her to be young and new and never named. You want her to be your first love, your first woman, you want her to be the whole of the earth. She knows it—for every woman is a concubine, a mistress of passion, a dompter of man's condition—and she becomes virginal and simple and, Lord, so new, so perfumed, that the ichor rises in the elephant, and you are at it again. (163)

The passage is the most sensual in the text. Woman as "a concubine, a mistress of passion, a dompter of man's condition" is a complete contrast to woman as Sita to Rama, Radha to Krishna, and woman as the meaning of the word, the breath, touch and act. These disparate views about the place of a woman in a man's life need not be construed as a kind of mess in which the narrator gets stuck. If we invoke the non-dualistic perspective from which Ramaswamy evaluates his experience, we may say that he is in a state of illusion. He talks about the eternity, the absolute, and the ineffable. His relationship with his wife, with Savithri, with Lakshmi, with Little Mother, and with Saroja lands him in a paradox, which he explains to Savithri:

> "Krishna is not Krishna yet. And when he is Krishna there is no Radha as Radha, but Radha is himself. That is the paradox,

Savithri, the mortal paradox of man."

"And the paradox is the fever. Lord, what would I not give that this fever should go, this fever that is me ... Lord, take me, and let me forget the world."

"Savithri, who can take whom? As I once told Madeleine, there where we take there is no love and there where we love there is no taking. You can but take yourself."

"Quickly then. How can it be achieved?"

"By—by discipleship," I answered, as though I was communicating my ultimate secret.

"Discipleship of what—to whom?"

"Discipleship of Krishna, of the Truth." (363)

The passage clearly dramatizes the ambivalence that is ubiquitous in the text. The ambivalence consists in the narrator's lack of confidence to affirm or deny. This amounts to a simple acceptance of one's dependence on a Guru, whose lantern shows the "long, white road." (335) We may make use of the usual critical cliches like the quest for identity, the East-West encounter, the image of India, and so on in our eagerness to squeeze the essence of *The Serpent and the Rope*. When an interlocutor asked Raja Rao, "In *The Serpent and the Rope* one of the central concerns seems to be 'the quest for identity'. Is it an existentialist influence?" Raja Rao replied, "No, *The Serpent and the Rope* is, primarily, a novel of 'quest for the absolute.'"[16] The quest for the absolute doesn't reach any consummation. On the other hand, we only see the continents combining and shifting, a sort of cross-cultural current flowing as if to no destination, while memory recalls and repeats the past experience of the narrator, sometimes evaluating the experience and sometimes processing it through a paradox. In other words, the narrator talking about illusion makes it a problematic—the serpent or the rope. It is only towards the end that we notice, in one of the excerpts of his diary, the narrator saying that

> This happened, this happened so long ago—Oh, as long ago as I have known myself be. Ever since being has known itself as being I have known it. It is the gift that Yagnyavalkya made

to Maiteryi, it is the gift Govinda made to Sri Sankara. It is the gift He made to me, my Lord. May I be worthy of the Lord. Lord, My Master! O thou abode of Truth. (403)

The narrator's discursive meditations end. The serpent and the rope disappear. The illusion that it is a quest in which he is involved melts, and the self beholds the vast space and the inexplicable silence.

If we compare Ramakrishna Pai of *The Cat and Shakespeare* with Ramaswamy, we can notice a subtle contrast. The vision that Ramakrishna Pai earns towards the end is characterized by the dissolution of the serpent and the rope, so that he could sing and be silent at one and the same time. The image of the cat carrying its kitten from place to place is significatory of *marjaranyaya*, according to which the absolute and the individual are two different spiritual entities and it is only implicit devotion and faith that would place the individual in the joyous realm of the absolute. Ramaswamy's Advaita, on the other hand, waits for the gift a master may give to the disciple. *The Cat and Shakespeare* and *The Serpent and the Rope* present a world which is not unreal but which is subject to a constant change. As a Western critic rightly points out, "What Shankara means . . . is that the world is an illusion in that it changes. God is not subject to change and thus is not an illusion in that Being is a constant (energy is conserved), though it is arguable that God's self-knowledge is capable of some undiscussable quality of process. To be illusory means to change, and to change means to exist in time. To be illusory, then, means to exist in time. Absolute Being must be extra-temporal. Obviously, our world is temporal, although the infinitesimal instant may somehow be congruent with eternity. We cannot say (in terms; that is, with inherently temporal fragments; that is, from a mortal perspective) just how the unillusory eternal is with us, unchanging, 'while' we are in time—but it is entirely possible that that is the case."[17] Making use of the brilliant insight embodied in the statement, we may say that the texts we have been discussing, while dramatizing the ongoing socio-political and cultural changes that are generated by various ideologies and a fusion of cultures, make it possible for the reader to see what is constant and unchanging in terms of the self. The truth of this observation can easily be illustrated by analyzing *Kanthapura.*

No doubt, *Kanthapura* captures the quintessence of India's rural life and its socio-cultural milieu. But the story of the village folk is narrated by an old lady, who often makes use of the plural "we," suggesting, thereby, the importance of the community and not the individual. The village has a Brahmin quarter, a Potters's quarter, a Weavers's quarter, a Sudra quarter, and a Pariah quarter. The inhabitants of the Brahmin quarter generally don't visit the Pariah quarter. The narrator tells us, "Of course you wouldn't expect me to go to the Pariah quarter, but I have seen from the street-corner Beadle Timmayya's hut."[18] Before the advent of the Gandhian social revolution, caste system dominates the village life. How rigid it is we can infer from the following passage:

> as he goes up the steps something in him says "Nay," and his hair stands on end as he remembers the tumbler of milk and the Pariah home, and so he calls out, "Rangamma, Rangamma!" and Rangamma says, "I'm coming," and when she is at the threshold, he says he has for the first time entered a pariah house and asks if he is permitted to enter; and Rangamma says, "Just come the other way round, Moorthy, and there's still hot water in the cauldron and fresh clothes for the meal." So Moorthy goes by the backyard, and when he has taken his bath and clothed himself, Rangamma says, "May be you'd better change your holy thread," but Moorthy says, "Now that I must go there every day, I cannot change my holy thread every day, can I?" and Rangamma says only, "I shall at least give you a little Ganges water, and you can take a spoonful of it each time you've touched them, can't you?" So Moorthy says, "As you will," and taking the Ganges water he feels a fresher breath flowing through him, and lest anyone should ask about his new adventure, he goes to the riverside after dinner to sit and think and pray. *After all a brahmin is a brahmin,* sister! (107, emphasis added)

From our point of view, the above passage brings to a central focus the sociological forces that have generated the Indian novel in English. Would a Brahmin lose his Brahminhood if he touches a pariah? Or, if a pariah touches a Brahmin, what would happen to the pariah and the Brahmin? These are the questions that have brought into Indian writing in English a novel like *Untouchable* and a poem like M. Krishna Murthy's "The Harijan."[19] We may include Raja Rao's *Kanthapura* in this category. Moorthy, the central character in *Kanthapura,* cannot change his holy thread everyday and cannot wash himself with the Ganges water because he has taken upon himself the task of spreading the gospel of Gandhi, which dissolves all castes into one caste. In this respect, Moorthy's opponent is Bhatta, the Brahmin money-lender, who opposes any truck with the pariahs. He tells Rangamma:

> Listen! Do you know Advocate Rama Sastri, the son of the old, orthodox Ranga Sastri, has now been talking of throwing open his temple to the pariahs? "The public temples are under the Government," he says, "but this one was built by my ancestors and I shall let the pariahs in, and which bastard of his father will say no?" I hope, however, the father will have croaked before that. But really aunt, we live in a strange age. What with their modern education and their modern women. Do you know, in the city they already have grown-up girls, fit enough to be mothers of two or three children, going to the Universities? And they talk to this boy and that boy; and what they do amongst themselves, heaven alone knows. And one, too, I heard, went and married a Mohomedan. Really, aunt, that is horrible! (43)

This passage suggests the fears of orthodox Brahmins like Bhatta that social changes would not only pollute society but may destroy the sanctity of the Hindu *dharma.* When Bhatta visits the city, Seetharamu tells him,

> The Swami is worried over this pariah movement, and he wants to crush it in its seed, before its cactus-roots have spread

> far and wide. You are a Bhatta and your voice is not a sparrow voice in your village, and you should speak to your people and organize a brahmin party. Otherwise brahminism is as good as kitchen ashes. The Mahatma is a good man and a simple man. But he is making too much of these carcass-eating pariahs. Toady it will be the pariahs, tomorrow it will be the Mohomedans, and the day after the Europeans. . . . We must stop this. The Swami says he will outcast every brahmin who has touched a pariah. That is the right way to begin. (44-45)

Not only do the Brahmins oppose the pariahs, but they rebuke Moorthy for his familiarity with Ratna, because Ratna is a young widow and her place is in the kitchen. As we read the narrative, we notice that Brahmin orthodoxy slowly but steadily loses ground and the spirit of Gandhi's gospel gains the upper hand. When the *satyagraha* movement is in full swing, Ratna's place in society as a freedom fighter is fully acknowledged, and all the women of Kanthapura say, "she is our chief now." (225) As *satyagrahis*, the women of Kanthapura break the age-old restrictions and taboos and become one. The following amply demonstrates this:

> Ratna blew the conch from the top of the Promontory, and with the blowing of the conch rose the *Satyanarayan Maharaj ki jai! Satyanarayan Maharaj ki jai!* from Swami's courtyard, and the throne was lifted up, and we marched through the Brahmin Street and the Potters' Street and the Pariah Street and the Weavers' Street and the doors creaked and children ran down the steps, and trays were in their hands, and the camphor was lit and the coconuts broken and the fruits offered, and one by one behind their mothers their grand-mothers and grand-aunts, and people said, "Sister, let me hold the torch. Sister, let me hold the sacred fan." And shoulder after shoulder changed beneath the procession-throne, and the cries of *Satyanarayan Maharaj ki jai! Satyanarayan Maharaj ki jai!* leapt into the air. And somebody said, "Let's sing `The Road to the City of love'," and we said "That's beautiful," and we clapped our hands and we sang, "The Road to the City of

Love is hard, brother." (234-35)

All have a place in the City of Love but the road to the City of Love is hard. The socio-cultural change that *Kanthapura* dramatizes is to be construed as a sort of liberation of the spirit. It is in this context that Ramaswamy's definition of a Brahmin as one who knows Brahman becomes meaningful; a Brahmin is not simply one who wears a holy thread but a pilgrim to the City of Love. Moorthy makes a beginning and the pilgrimage ends in the vision of Ramakrishna Pai in *The Cat and Shakespeare.*

Padmanabha Iyer alias Comrade Kirillov seeks liberation through the Marxian dialectic. He learns German to read Marx and Engels. Though he has no faith in the gospel of Gandhi, Kirillov owes his innate honesty to his ancient tradition and culture. The narrator of *Comrade Kirillov* wonders, "How alike, I thought to myself, my Sanyasi of Benares, and this Sadhu of Communism."[20] But the explanation for the fusion of the Sadhu and the Communist in Kirillov the narrator himself gives at a later point. When the narrator asks him the reason for reciting a verse from Sankara, he says that "just as St. Francis was a great poet, Sankara was a greater one. I think Rajasekhara in the ninth-century quotes Sankara to prove some abstruse theory in poetics. I have forgotten the exact text. I love Sankara. I love his Nirvana Astaka. Come, Come, let us sing it together.' '*Manobuddhi ahankara cittani naham/ cidananda rupa shivoham-shivoham*' (I am not the mind, I am neither intelligence nor egoism,/ I am joy of intelligence—I am Shiva, I am Shiva)."[21]

From the foregoing analysis, a few interesting points emerge. Raja Rao's fictions by and large have metaphysical overtones. His protagonists—Moorthy, Ramaswamy, Ramakrishna Pai, and Kirillov alias Padmanabha Iyer—are all Brahmins. Their awareness of the sanctity and the profundity of the Brahmin (the *Vedic*) view of life is indisputable. Their degree and level of awareness differ, but their constant preoccupation seems to be to earn and evaluate sometimes a glimpse and sometimes a vision of the ineffable ("I am joy of intelligence—I am Shiva, I am Shiva"). They strive to authenticate this experience of the self not as isolated or self-exiled individuals (as the nineteenth-century American transcendentalists, especially Emerson and Whitman, did) but as members of a society nourished and nurtured by a metaphysics which consists in a realization that smashes all categories and transcends political, national, and linguistic limitations.

NOTES

1. B. Rajan, *The Dark Dancer*, p. 167.
2. Raja Rao, *The Serpent and the Rope* (Delhi: Hind Pocket Books, 1968), p. 5.
3. Raja Rao, *The Cat and Shakespeare* (Delhi: Hind Pocket Books, 1971), p. 38.
4. M.K. Naik, *Raja Rao* (Twayne's World Authors Series, 234, New York: Twayne, 1972), p. 126.
5. D.H. Lawrence, "The Novel," *Phoenix II: Uncollected, Unpublished, and Other Prose Works by D.H. Lawrence*, ed. Warren Roberts and Harry T. Moore (1968; rpt. New York: Penguin Books, 1978), p. 426.
6. William Shakespeare, *Much Ado About Nothing,* V, i, 204-208, *William Shakespeare: The Complete Works,* ed. Peter Alexander (1951; rpt. London: Collins, 1960).
7. William Shakespeare, *Hamlet*, I, iv, 90.
8. William Shakespeare, *A Midsummer-Night's Dream*, V, i, 12-22.
9. Jorge Luis Borges, "Everything and Nothing," trans. James E. Irby, *Labyrinths: Selected Stories and Other Writings*, ed. Donald A. Yates and James E. Irby (1964; rpt. Harmondsworth: Penguin Books, 1981), p. 285.
10. Shiva Niranjan, "An Interview with Raja Rao," *Indian Writing in English*, ed. Krishna Nandan Sinha (New Delhi: Heritage, 1979), p. 25.
11. *Ibid.*, p. 20.
12. Swami Chidbhavananda, trans., *The Bhagavad Gita* (Tirupparaitturai: Tapovanam, 1965), p. 52.
13. Dorrit Cohn, *Transparent Minds: Narrative Modes for Presenting Consciousness in Fiction* (Princeton: Princeton University Press, 1978), p. 144.

14. Shiva Niranjan, p. 20.
15. Shyamala A. Narayan, "Ramaswamy's Erudition: A Note on Raja Rao's *The Serpent and the Rope*," *ARIEL*, XIV, No. 4 (October 1983), p. 10.
16. Asha Kaushik, "Meeting Raja Rao," *The Literary Criterion* (Mysore), XVIII, No.3 (1983), p. 36.
17. Bruce F. Kawin, *The Mind of the Novel: Reflexive Fiction and the Ineffable* (Princeton: Princeton University Press, 1982), pp. 126-27.
18. Raja Rao, *Kanthapura* (New Delhi: Orient Paperbacks, 1971), p. 13.
19. M. Krishna Murthy, "The Harijan," *The Peacock Lute: Anthology of Poems in English by Indian Writers*, ed. V.N. Bhushan (Bombay: Padma., 1945), p. 73.
20. Raja Rao, *Comrade Kirillov* (New Delhi: Orient Paperbacks, 1976), pp. 71-72.
21. *Ibid.*, p. 86.

Narayan and the Comedy of the Self

R.K. Narayan is pre-eminently a story-teller. His stories are not only interesting in themselves but are very suggestive, in the sense that they are a creative comment on contemporary reality. But, given the Indian context, it is not a simple affair to decide what is contemporary and what is perennial. In *Reluctant Guru*, Narayan says, "a novel is about an individual living his life in a world imagined by the author, performing a set of actions (upto a limit) contrived by the author. But to take a work of fiction as a sociological study or a social document could be very misleading. My novel *The Guide* was not about the saints or the pseudo-saints of India, but about a particular person."[1] Here Narayan suggests how his fictions have to be construed and evaluated. The emphasis is on the individual (character) and action. Character and action are meaningful within the framework (plot) the author creates. A cursory glance at the captions of his fictions re-inforces the point. *Swami and Friends, The Bachelor of Arts, The English Teacher, Mr. Sampath, The Financial Expert, The Guide, The Vendor of Sweets*, and *The Painter of Signs* do suggest that Narayan envisions a character and gives him a name and a local habitation. His protagonists perform functions which have social and individual signficance. In the following pages, the critical focus is on the way his protagonists fulfil their obligations to themselves and to others. The process of realizing one's self through a network of socio-cultural institutions is the staple reality we notice in the fictions of Narayan. In this context, we have to be cautious in applying the canons of Western realism in determining and evaluating the contours and the significance of Narayan's fictions. The Western view of realism and realistic literature is very cogently described by J.P. Stern:

> The riches of the represented world, its weightiness and resistance to ideals; its consequential logic and circumstantiality—these I take to be among the attributes one would expect to find in realistic literature.[2]

Narayan's views on reality and realism are not entirely different from those of Stern. But he has made realism pretty Indian by making it more inclusive and thoroughly traditional, as the following passage amply demonstrates:

> Even the legends and myths, as contained in the *puranas*, of which there are eighteen major ones, are mere illustrations of the moral and spiritual truths enunciated in the *Vedas*. "No one can understand the significance of any story in our mythology unless he is deeply versed in the *Vedas*," the story-teller often declares. Everything is interrelated. Stories, scriptures, ethics, philosophy, grammar, astrology, astronomy, semantics, mysticism, and moral codes—each forms part and parcel of a total life and is indispensable for the attainment of a four-square understanding of existence. Literature is not a branch of study to be placed in a separate compartment, for the edification only of scholars, but a comprehensive and artistic medium of expression to benefit the literate and the illiterate alike. A true literary composition should appeal in an infinite variety of ways; any set of stanzas of the *Ramayana* could be set to music and sung, narrated with dialogue and action and treated as the finest drama, studied analytically for an understanding of the subtleties of language and grammar, or distilled finely to yield esoteric truths.[3]

The centrality of the above citation in making sense of Narayan's stories need not be exaggerated. In Narayan's realism, everything is interrelated. The world of Narayan the story-teller is not a series of scenes and characters but a composite and organic whole in which "each forms part and parcel of a total life and is indispensable for the attainment of a four-square understanding of existence." "The attainment of a four-square understanding of existence'' doesn't mean that Narayan is an existentialist. Like Raja Rao, he draws his creative sustenance from his cultural past and a very steady and subtle awareness of the present.

The above may be illustrated by analyzing any text of Narayan. For the sake of expository convenience, let us consider *The Financial Expert.* The narrative proceeds from a single point of view, that of Margayya. The following is a good illustration of the way in which Margayya's mind works towards a goal which he postulates for himself:

> Margayya's blood was completely the city man's and revelled in crowds, noise and bustle; the moment he looked out and saw the stream of people and traffic flowing up and down the road, he felt that he was in the right place. A poet would perhaps have felt exasperated by the continuous din, but to Margayya it was like a background music to his own thoughts. There was a row of offices and shops opposite, insurance agencies, local representatives of newspapers, hair-cutting saloons, some film distributors, a lawyer's chamber, and hardware shop, into which hundreds of people were going every day. Margayya calculated that if he could at least filter twenty out of that number for his own purposes, he would be more than well off. In about a year he could pass on to the grade of people who were wealthy and not merely rich. He drew a lot of distinction between the two. A rich man, according to his view, was just one caste below the man of wealth. Riches any hard-working fool could attain by some watchfulness, while acquiring wealth was an extraordinarily specialized job. It came to persons who had on them the grace of the Goddess fully and who could use their wits. He was a specialist in money and his mind always ran on lines of scientific enquiry whenever money came in question. He differentiated with great subtlety between money, riches, wealth, and fortune. It was most important people should not mistake one for the other.[4]

The above passage brings out Margayya's shrewdness and his

capacity to think ahead of the situation in which he is involved. Margayya is a man of the city, and a city is the place where one can make a fortune. For him, reality consists in offices, shops, insurance agencies, newspaper agencies, lawyers's chambers and hair-cutting saloons, to which hundreds of people come and go every day. The distinction he makes between riches and wealth brings to the fore a kind of caste system which streamlines the narrative. Any fool can become rich if he is watchful and hard-working. But acquiring wealth is "an extraordinarily specialized job." Apart from "the grace of the Goddess," one has to use one's "wits" to acquire wealth. The nice distinction he makes between money, riches, wealth, and fortune suggests that he makes a good use of his wits. But it also suggests that the goddess of wealth is a very vacillating one, and Margayya, in spite of his wits, miscalculates "the grace of the Goddess." If the reader watches the curve of Margayya's development from money to riches, and from riches to wealth, he can anticipate the end. The ending of the narrative ironically places Margayya in the beginning, so that one may say that the end is embryonically contained in the beginning. In talking about the beginnings and the endings of narratives, we have to be careful and should not associate them with Eliot's well-known lines in *Four Quartets*.[5] What we have been trying to suggest is the fluctuation of fortune we notice in Narayan's stories. The ironic perspective in Narayan's stories, or the ironic vision of Narayan, is meaningful only in terms of character in action, which has reference to the plot of the story, in the sense that a story is sequential whereas a plot is both sequential and consequential. In *The Financial Expert*, Margayya's action is tenaciously oriented to the acquisition of money, which would make him rich and later place him in the caste of the wealthy. But, curiously enough, the fluctuating fortune plays its crucial role and drives home the point that the goddess of wealth is a very vacillating one. It is in this sense that Narayan's narratives are generically comic. The essence of comedy consists in progressing from an obsessive illusion to an equally debilitating disillusion, which would land one on the sober strand of truth. We shall discuss this point in detail when we sum up the significance of the self, the family, and society in Narayan.

The narrative opens with a semantic exploration of the protagonist's name, Margayya: "Marga" means the way and "Ayya" is an honorific suffix. The narrator tells us that Margayya means one who shows the way. Margayya shows the way out to those in financial trouble. Margayya uses his wit to undermine the foundations of the co-operative movement; he shows the peasants an easy way to draw unlimited loans from the co-operative bank, without committing themselves to repay the loans. When the authorities of the bank object to his nefarious activities, he turns his mind to various other ways of earning money. The word "money" runs through the narrative like a refrain. For example, Margayya tells his wife, "Even you will learn to behave with me when I have money." (17) The narrator tells us, "As he went through the town that day he was obsessed with thoughts of money. His mind rang with the words he had said to the villagers: 'I am only trying to help you to get out of your money worries.' He began to believe it himself." (21) Margayya tells the priest in the temple, "I want to acquire wealth. Can you show me a way? I will do anything you suggest." (29) He thinks that "there is a lot of money" (68) in manufacturing soaps. After the successful publication and sale of the copies of *Domestic Harmony* (or *Bed Life*), the narrator comments: "The business always seemed to him an alien one. The only interesting thing about it seemed to be the *money* that was coming in. 'But *money* is not everything,' he told himself one day. It was a very strange statement to come from a person like Margayya. But if he had been asked to explain or expand it further, he would have said: '*Money* is very good no doubt, but the whole thing seems to be in a wrong setting'." (94-95, emphasis added) Illustrations can be multiplied, but the point to be noted is Margayya's scruples. In his anxiety to place money in a right setting, he sells his share in *Domestic Harmony* to the printer, Mr. Lal. He tells his wife, "Did you ever notice how I have managed not to bring a single copy into this house? I don't want our Balu even to know that there is such a book." (95) In the same breath, he also tells her, "I don't want people to say that Balu enjoys all the money earned through *Domestic Harmony*. I would do anything to avoid it." (95) It is precisely here that a calculating person like Margayya miscalculates the significance of *Domestic*

Harmony. When Balu and his wife shift to their new house, Dr Pal, the author of *Domestic Harmony*, visits them frequently. Under the expert supervision of Dr Pal, Balu puts the aesthetic of *Domestic Harmony* into practice. Margayya loses his temper and beats Dr Pal for corrupting his son. In order to wreak vengeance on Margayya, Dr Pal encourages and incites Margayya's clients to withdraw their deposits along with interest from Margayya's bank, which makes Margayya ultimately insolvent.

Margayya, the financial expert, acquires money, riches, and wealth through the good offices of Dr Pal, the author of *Domestic Harmony*. Since fortune, in principle, constantly fluctuates, we find Margayya's rise and fall caused by a reversal which can be located in the plot of *The Financial Expert*. *Domestic Harmony*, paradoxically enough, brings domestic disharmony into Margayya's household. It creates a cleavage between the father and the son, between the wife and the husband, between the self and society. Margayya's hasty and miscalculated assault on Dr Pal acts as a reverse gear and takes Margayya back to the banyan tree in front of the co-operative bank. Margayya's rise and fall do not make him a cynic. On the other hand, they make him perhaps more sober than we see him earlier. Expressing his eagerness to have his grandson with him, he says, "I will play with him. Life has been too dull without him in this house." (178) Margayya's last words in their casual tone and relaxed ring, offer the essence of domestic harmony, which heals the breach between the self and society.

The Vendor of Sweets and *The Financial Expert* have a similar structural pattern, more or less. In both, narration proceeds from a single point of view. Both Jagan and Margayya are worshippers of the goddess Lakshmi. Margayya's orientation towards the problems of the self is largely mundane. Jagan is an improvement over Margayya, in the sense that he appears to be very cultivated, has faith and sympathy, and maintains happy relationship with his servants, businessmen, and friends. Margayya's one problem is his son Balu. He takes all the necessary care to educate his son. In a room specially arranged for Balu's studies, Margayya keeps a framed picture of the goddess Saraswati, so that his son may have the blessings of the goddess in his pursuit of academic ambitions.

Jagan keeps a framed picture of the goddess Lakshmi and starts his business day by placing a string of jasmine on the top of the frame. But he seems to have no special reverence for the goddess of learning. His son Mali, like Margayya's son, Balu, becomes a thorn in his flesh. The plot of both the texts is built with the father-son relationship as the corner-stone—in such a way that when the relationship reaches a crisis, there is a sudden fluctuation in the fortunes of the protagonists. It is here that one notices the comic structuration that is built into the text. As a theorist on the comic mode in fiction says, "Repetition is comic; an unexpected break in that repetition is more so; and best of all is recognition of a pattern that comprehends them both. The theory of incongruity goes far toward explaining comedy but stops short of the best sort, in which the incongruous is finally seen to be congruent to a larger pattern than that which was originally perceived."[6] The incongruity we notice in Margayya's propitiation of the goddess of learning and the goddess of wealth becomes a more inclusive pattern in Jagan, who repeatedly talks about the Gandhian ethic and the *Gita*, and says, "Money is an evil" and "We should be happier without it,"[7] and at the same time hoards currency in an attic and very meticulously counts cash in the sweet-shop.

Jagan, whom we see as a complacent and self-satisfied owner of the sweet-shop, seems to lose his sense of sweetness and light when Mali tells him, "I can't study any more." (29) The narrator tells us: "He was a cowardly father and felt afraid to mention class or college. The boy might scream at their mention or kick away his breakfast." (30) Although he retains "a vestige of conscience from his days of public service," (31) he often grumbles to distribute sweets to the school children that pass by his shop. At the same time he feels very apologetic to sit in the shop, collecting the cash. It is his inability to face his own problems squarely that lands him sometimes in comic and sometimes in serious situations. When his cousin tells him that Mali wants to be a writer, he feels uneasy, because in his dictionary "writer" means "clerk." As he gets more information regarding his son's ambitions and activities, he thinks that his son wants to be a Shakespeare or a Kalidasa. He tells his cousin, "College or no college, I know Kalidasa was a village idiot and a shepherd until the goddess Saraswati made a scratch on his tongue and then he burst into that song *Syamala-dandakam*, and wrote *Sakuntala* and so on. I know the story. I have heard it often enough." (38) Though he knows the story of Kalidasa, he doesn't bestow much faith on its message. His fondness for his son and the strong mental image of his dead wife make all sweetness evaporate from the life of the vendor of sweets. No doubt, he tries to make it up with his son by avoiding words like college, classes, and education, but strong doubts oppress his mind, and in spite of his best efforts, he cannot completely identify himself with his son's fantasies. Some time later, when his cousin tells him that Mali wants to go to America to learn the art of story-writing, he feels unnerved, and says, "Did Valmiki go to America or Germany in order to learn to write his *Ramayana*?" (51) He refuses to finance his son's visit to America. But Mali knows the place where Jagan keeps his cash. He takes ten thousand rupees from the hoarded bundles of currency and leaves for America. Compelled by circumstances and the pain of separation, Jagan looks forward to Mali's return from America. But Mali's return creates more problems for Jagan than he ever anticipated, because Mali brings from America a young woman about whose bonafides Jagan has innumerable doubts. He introduces her to his father, saying, "This is Grace. We are married. Grace, my dad." (64) This brief introduction creates complete confusion in Jagan's mind. The uncertainty becomes more acute when Mali tells him that he is interested in fabricating a story-writing machine, which requires large capital, about fifty thousand dollars. The following passages amply demonstrates the comic mode and the emerging irony of situation, which is a plot element in most fictions of Narayan:

> Fifty thousand dollars! Whatever its equivalent might be, it was a staggering sum. "I am a poor man," Jagan wailed, and immediately noticed the shock on Mali's face and the embarrassment he had created in the presence of Grace. It was as if he had uttered a bad word. Seeing this, Jagan said "Gandhi always advocated poverty and not riches."
>
> "And yet you earn your thousand rupees a day," said Mali

with a vicious smile.

"If you feel you can take up the business and run it, do so; it is yours if you want it."

"You expect me to do that? I have better plans than to be a vendor of sweetmeats." (95-96)

The recollection of the scene, he felt, would overwhelm him; he might break down and it would be silly to be seen in tears while he was occupying the throne. He had a mental picture of himself standing like a ragged petitioner in the presence of Mali and the Chinese girl, being sneered at for his business of a lifetime, a business that had provided the money for Mali to fly to America and do all sorts of things there. "Vendor of sweetmeats," indeed. (98)

The preceding passages very well exemplify the narrative mode Narayan usually employs. The confrontation between the father and the son reminds us of the confrontation in *The Financial Expert*, in which Balu demands a share in Margayya's property. Margayya's toughness as a man of the world helps him negotiate with the situation. But Jagan doesn't have Margayya's strength and tenacity, maybe owing to his lifelong association with the Gandhian ethic. While toughness makes Margayya talk and behave like a character in a novel by Meredith, Jagan's behaviour as an embodiment of passive resistance makes him no less comic. He seems to drown all his agonies in his shop, which is like a classroom, in which all his servants are his pupils, hearing his exposition on the *Bhagavat Gita*. It is in one of these mixed moods that he agrees to accompany the hair-blackener to Nallappa's Grove, where he is shown a marvellous sculpture of the goddess Gayatri in an unfinished state. The narrator comments: "Watching him (the hair-blackener) in this setting, it was difficult for Jagan, as he mutely followed him, to believe that he was in the twentieth century. Sweetmeat vending, money and his son's problems seemed remote and unrelated to him. The edge of reality itself was beginning to blur; this man from the previous millennium seemed to be the only object worth notice; he looked like one possessed." (118) But the problems—sweetmeat vending, money, and his son—do not vanish. While Margayya tries to face his domestic problems squarely, Jagan tries to escape from them, always keeping in his pocket his cheque book. He tries to console himself by saying, "At sixty, one is reborn and enters a new *janma.*" (182) His troubles come to an end when the police arrest Mali for keeping a bottle of alcohol in his car. When his cousin meets him in his retreat across the river, Jagan tells him, "A dose of prison life is not a bad thing. It may be just what he needs now." (191-92) Though he doesn't worry about his son's disgrace, he is anxious to provide money for Grace to buy a ticket to America. He thinks that it is a duty he owes to her.

The above critique of *The Vendor of Sweets* helps us in seeing how Narayan transmutes the story of Jagan, a sweetmeat vendor, into a comedy of the self. Though he tries to escape the problems that arise out of the familial and the social relations, he has the kind of awareness that, at least some times, clarifies his obligations towards the self, towards others, and towards society at large. The following passage very well exemplifies the observations we have just made:

> Jagan counted the cash and made the entries, but his mind worked on one theme only: the puzzle created by Mali. At every encounter he displayed a new facet, which might or might not have relevance to the previous one. Jagan was reminded of the concept of *Viswarupa* that he had read about in the *Bhagavat Gita.* When the warrior Arjuna hesitated to perform his duty on the battlefield, God came to him in guise of his charioteer and revealed Himself in all His immensity. On one side he was thousand-faced. "I behold You, infinite in forms on all sides, with countless arms, stomachs, mouths and eyes; neither Your end nor middle nor beginning do I see . . ." quoted Jagan inwardly, at the same time remaining rational enough to realize the irreverence of the comparison. (153)

The crucial concept here appears to be *Viswarupa.* In the sacred text, it symbolizes the material and the spiritual aspects of reality which is endless and timeless. In a way, it is co-terminus with the beginning and the end of life. At a lower level, it represents the world in which innumerable creatures, including man, are born, and they die, sometimes reaching the destined goal and sometimes falling like leaves from a tree in autumn. Whether Jagan is aware of the inclusive specificities of the sacred concept we may not be able to say; but his creator seems to be aware of this.

The world in which we live and its immense variety and multiplicity cannot be visualized and represented in a single creative moment. *The Painter of Signs* seems to suggest that even a signboard-painter who tries to present something in bold colours cannot trust the colours, because of the innumerable colour combinations that are available to him. In short, colours of reality often defy careful selection. The specifications of those who want signboards differ from the theoretical specifications of a signboard-painter. Raman, the signboard-painter, wants to establish the age of reason in the world. He declares his faith, saying, "I want a rational explanation for everything.... Otherwise my mind refuses to accept any statement.... I am a rationalist, and I don't do anything unless I see some logic in it."[8] If we look at the context in which Raman declares his faith, it becomes clear that logic is not a monolithic entity but a flexible tool that serves any number of minds to establish the rationality of their schemes and plans. The lawyer who orders a signboard wants Raman to employ slanting letters in writing the signboard. Raman tells him: "Slanting letters are suitable only for oil-merchants and soap-sellers," and adds: "The letters on a lawyer's board must always stand up proudly." (5) He thinks that logic justifies his assertion. The lawyer tells him, "What more logic do you want than that I am paying for it? And I want it that way and the slanting letters to be shaded; that's all there is to it." (5) The logic of the lawyer and that of the painter of signs are a part of *Viswarupa*, which doesn't exclude anything under the sun. But it takes more time for the protagonist of *The Painter of Signs* to realize it. Significantly enough, the painter of signs frequents The Boardless Hotel. In a town in which all thriving hotels have boards, even The Boardless Hotel has a roaring business. This suggests that reality, though people label it in different ways, doesn't need a label. Raman passes through a number of dramatic and funny situations before he can realize the significance of reality in his routine life. Like Margayya's world, Raman's world is that of hotel managers, businessmen, bangle sellers, lawyers, doctors, and others, whose minds are always preoccupied with cash. He is aware of the corrupt practices of his patrons. In The Boardless he meets his friend Gupta, who has a constant grouse against the government. But he doesn't contradict him because "Gupta gave him much work, as he started a new business under a new name each year in order to confound the sales tax, income tax, and all other governmental tax-devisers. Establishing a new enterprise meant only blacking out an old sign and writing a new one in its place, and he paid down five rupees per letter without a word. And he appreciated any one who refrained from contradicting his political views." (15) Raman has sufficient knack to negotiate with the Guptas of the world. But he also seems to suffer from distracting thoughts. The narrator tells us: "He wanted to get away from sex thoughts, minimize their importance, just as he wished to reduce the importance of money. Money and sex, he reflected, obsessive thoughts, too much everywhere—literature, magazines, drama, or cinema deal with nothing but sex all the time, but the female figure, water-soaked, is enchanting." (14)

The comic turn in the narrative takes the form of a female figure, Daisy, who commissions Raman to paint a signboard for the Family Planning Centre in Malgudi. His relationship with Daisy involves him in the problematic of sex which he has been trying to ignore and avoid.

If we analyze the Raman-Daisy relationship, we may be in a better position to spotlight and clarify the kind of comedy we have in *The Painter of Signs*. Daisy appears to Raman like "a minor dancer." (31) He has an urge to call on her and know from her why she calls herself Daisy. But his habitual self-criticism intervenes, and he feels: "To pursue a female after seeing only the upper half, above the desk—she might be one-legged, after all. But this is not sex which is driving me, but a normal curiosity about another person, that's all." (33) Even to satisfy his normal curiosity he feels shy, and thinks of the various ways in which he can introduce himself to Daisy. But his visit to Daisy makes him realize: "She seemed to know her mind and its limits.'' (35) But the poor fellow has prepared himself for this visit with the utmost care. The narrator tells us that he ''kept awake himself the night thinking of it; roused himself from dreams relevant and irrelevant to his mood, and dressed himself with care—a light yellow bush-coat and white trousers with the creases in perfect shape; shaved his chin to a gloss; combed his hair back, applying brilliantine.'' (35) The verbs—''roused,'' ''dressed,'' ''shaved,'' and ''combed''—chisel the figure of Raman in such a way that the image of Raman is always there not as a passionate lover but as one who is playing with the preliminaries of courtship. After satisfying his curiosity, he tries to parade his theoretical knowledge about signboard painting, so that he may fuse with Daisy's preoccupation with family planning. When he goes to her office to fix the signboard he has painted for the Family Planning Centre, mere curiosity is replaced by a dim hope that he may be able to cajole and persuade her to take more interest in him. She appears to be more reciprocative in the office than at her home. But he is, at the same time, restless as he always thought that a man has more important things to do in life. He feels: ''Mind conditioned by story-writers, poets, and dramatists from time immemorial who had no other theme than love—easiest subject to deal with. This philosophy had been my armour and made me unique all these years. Now am I on the verge of defeat?'' (45) The theme of love becomes so obsessive that he accepts defeat; in other words, he gives up the armour of a bachelor and puts on the armour of a lover. But he does not realize that Daisy has committed herself to a cause and her response to his shy and tacit looks is not love but sheer goodwill. Her dedication to the task of spreading the message of family planning, though seems to be complete, has a certain amount of exaggeration in it. She tells Raman repeatedly that the growth of population in India is India's greatest enemy, and he feels irksome. To cope with her zeal, ''He realized he had been mistaken in taking her to be just a suave bureaucrat who got signboards written and files completed and properly knotted with red-tape while within she seemed to carry a furnace of conviction.'' (57)

Raman tours a number of villages along with Daisy to paint

family planning signs ana symbols on walls, if it is necessary. Wherever she goes, she meets with resistance from the villagers, who are indifferent to the entire idea of family planning. But this does not in any way affect Daisy's zeal to propagate the message. In one of the villages Raman comes across a Brahmin priest who tells him that he can tame and subdue a man-eater. In fact, he did it once, when the villagers were shivering with fear as an old tiger was roaming round the village. Of course, one may see here the seed of a later fiction of Narayan, *A Tiger for Malgudi.* But Raman is not interested in the charming power of the old man. Forgetting his aim to establish the age of reason, he prostrates before the image of the goddess the old man worships, and mumbles, "May Daisy be mine without further delay. I can't live without her." (77) But the goddess seems to have other thoughts. She probably knows that Raman and Daisy cannot pull together. On their return journey to Malgudi, they travel in a bullock cart. The cartman thinks that they are wife and husband. Raman keeps quiet while Daisy says, "Make no mistake. We are not married." (99) When they meet again, Daisy tells him her own story. She comes from a joint family. The household is like a hostel, consisting of innumerable children and adults. When a prospective bridegroom came to see her, she refused to appear before him. Though she yielded to the pressures of her family, she behaved in an erratic fashion before the groom. When the members of her family scolded her for her behaviour, she escaped from the village.

At no point in their relationship does Daisy allow Raman to take liberties with her. He feels that he is overburdened by and drowned in "Daisy-ism." But the relationship doesn't end there. He still entertains hopes of marrying Daisy. When his aunt, before leaving for Benares, asks him when and how he is getting married to Daisy, he tells her that it will be a very simple ceremony. But this simple ceremony doesn't take place. Daisy always puts off the day, and she leaves Malgudi. Just before her departure, when Raman asks her, "you have shown a tremendous storehouse of the love, you can give a fellow new life; why do you want to kill that great gift within you?" she tells him, "Because I have a different life chalked out." (180-81) When Daisy is about to leave Malgudi in Gaffur's taxi, the following dialogue ensues between Raman and Gaffur:

> "Take the ladies safely. Just a moment, Gaffur, you know what I feel like doing now?'
>
> "Yes, Ram, good to see you. What do you want to do?"
>
> "Drive a nail into your tyre."
>
> "Always boyish! Why?"
>
> "I don't know. Don't ask for reasons. Goodbye, ladies." He cried, as Gaffur's ancient chevrolet roared and belched smoke and jerked forward. (183)

Raman's words in the above dialogue, though have a touch of resentment, are on the whole humorous. Though a rationalist, curiously enough, now he refuses to rationalize. The narrator tells us, "He mounted his cycle and turned towards The Boardless—that solid, real world of sublime souls who minded their own business." (183) Several times Raman offers to write a signboard for The Boardless Hotel, but the proprietor resists the offer. The Boardless, according to the narrator, is the solid and real world, which suggests that reality is without a label; it is the self that is eager to paint a signboard for reality. It is in this process of naming, the self realizes, that naming has limited scope and narrow significance. Most values are only within and seldom find their appropriate objective correlatives. To come to a case in point, we see Raman getting involved in "Daisy-ism," for which Daisy is not the objective correlative. Sometimes illusion may take the form of a staple object for which there may be a signboard. But signboards are not significatory of what is real. What is real is not easy to define or explicate; it is boardless. In this context, the sublime virtue consists in one's minding one's own business. It is this that Raju in *The Guide* fails to do. This point becomes clear if we compare Rosie with Daisy. Both of them dedicate themselves to a value that is impersonal. Just as to Daisy spreading the message of family planning among people who are indifferent to it is a means and not an end in itself, to Rosie dancing is only a means to achieve the poise of the self rather than an end in itself. Just as Raman fails to understand the nature of Daisy, Raju misinterprets the character of Rosie and what she wants in life, in spite of many hints and suggestions she frequently gives. Daisy tells Raman, just before her departure, "At some moments, and moods, we say and do things—like talking in sleep, but when you awake, you realize your folly. . . . Oh, forgive me for misleading you." (180) In *The Guide*, Rosie tells Raju, when he proposes a brief holiday, "I don't think it's going to be possible until I fall sick or break my thigh bone. . . . Do you know the bulls yoked to an oil-crusher—they keep going round and round and round, in a circle, without a beginning or an end?"[9] A few moments later Raju, trying to dispel her doubts, tells her, "As far as I can see, there is nothing for you to be sorry about—you are famous, you have made money, you do what you like. You wanted to dance; you have done it." (181) But Rosie's reply contains her ironic assessment of herself: "Till the thought of it makes me sick. . . . I feel like one of those parrots in a cage taken around village-fairs, or a performing monkey, as he used to say." (181) Ultimately, when the superintendent arrests Raju, he requests him to give him some time so that he can inform Rosie. He expects and thinks that his arrest would make her sob, but she merely tells him, "I felt all along you were not doing right things. This is *Karma*. What can we do?" (193) This reminds us of Daisy's words to Raman: "I have a different life chalked out. . . . Do me this great favour—don't again talk of thc past or think of it. I am wiping it out from my mind. I can." (181)

The foregoing citations from *The Painter of Signs* and *The Guide* bracket together Rosie and Daisy. The comedy in these two texts issues from the incongruity the protagonists and the reader notice in the codes that propel their behaviours. Unnerved by Rosie's fluctuating moods of self-pity and submissiveness, Raju feels: "I couldn't understand her. I had an appalling thought that for months and months I had eaten, slept, and lived with her, without in the least understanding her mind. What were her moods? Was she sane or insane? Was she a liar? Did she bring all these charges against her husband at our first meeting just to seduce me? Would she be levelling various charges against me now that she seemed to be tiring of me—even to the extent of saying that I was a moron and an imbecile? I felt bewildered and unhappy. I didn't understand her sudden affection for her husband. What was this sudden mood that was coming over her? I did my best for her. Her career was at its height. What was it that still troubled her? Could I get at it and find a remedy? I had been taking too much for granted in our hectic professional existence.'' (180) May be in their hectic professional existence Raju fails to interpret rightly her self-pity, her renewed admiration for her husband, and the import of the images like ''the bulls yoked to an oil-cusher,'' ''one of those parrots in a cage,'' and ''a performing monkey.''

From the above analysis, we are not wrong in inferring that, like Raman the painter of signs, Raju is a poor guide of his self, though he may be an enthusiastic tourist guide to people like Rosie and Marco. As the fame and name of Rosie spread far and wide, and her talent finds good market, Raju feels that he has acquired some status in society. Apart from this illusion he entertains, he says, ''I resented any one wanting to make a direct approach to her. She was my property. This idea was beginning to take root in my mind.'' (168) Coupled with this passion to possess everything, he seems to suffer from an inexplicable over-confidence in his capacity to guide others. Moreover, as the narrrator says, ''It was in his nature to get involved in other people's interests and activities.'' (8) Raju himself confesses and often reflects: ''Otherwise... I should have grown up like a thousand other normal persons, without worries in life.'' (8)

The narration in *The Guide* proceeds at two levels. Raju narrates the story of his life to Velan. When his disciples, the village folk, prevail on him to face the ordeal of standing knee-deep in water without food for propitiating the god of rain, Raju confesses to Velan by narrating his story. This we notice in Section Six of the text. Sections Seven, Eight, Nine, and Ten constitute Raju's free and frank confession of his past experiences and lapses. The concluding section dramatizes Raju's efforts to live up to the expectations of the image of himself he has raised in the minds of the village folk. In the first six sections, we have the narrator and Raju alternately narrating, so that the narrative voice may be taken as a chorus that enlarges and specifies the scope and the significance of what Raju has to say about himself and his activities. The narrative begins as follows:

> Raju welcomed the intrusion—something to relieve the loneliness of the place. The man stood gazing reverentially on his face. Raju felt amused and embarrassed. "Sit down if you like," Raju said, to break the spell. The other accepted the suggestion with a grateful nod and went down the river steps to wash his feet and face, came up wiping himself dry with the end of a chequered yellow towel on his shoulder and took his seat two steps below the granite slab on which Raju was sitting cross-legged as if it were a throne, beside an ancient shrine. (5)

The above passage conveys the feel and the spirit of the rest of the narrative. The granite slab on which Raju sits assumes the position of a throne, suggesting that to the villagers he will be a Maharaja, because sometimes the rural folk address a saint as Maharaja. The man who intrudes gazes at Raju's face "reverentially." Whether his face really inspires reverence in the onlooker or not need not trouble us. But the point to be noted is that it amuses and embarrasses Raju. The words "spell" and "shrine," while suggesting the man's veneration for what is sacred, make the reader ponder and feel uncertain when the narrator says, "the villager resumed the study of his face with intense respect. And Raju stroked his chin thoughtfully to make sure that an apostolic beard had not suddenly grown there. It was still smooth. He had had his last shave only two days before and paid for it with the hard-earned coins of his jail life." (6) The narrator doesn't leave the reader in any doubt whatsoever regarding Raju's bonafides. But he does suggest that Raju's face has a certain bewitching charm that accounts for some of his troubles. This impression is reinforced by the words of the barber who gives a shave to Raju after his release from jail: "you look like a *maharaja* now." (8) It may not be a far-fetched inference to see an ironic link between Raju and Maharaja because the story of Raju's past, narrated as a flash-back, confirms the pattern that the narrator's remarks quoted earlier suggest. The problem that Velan tries to place before Raju for his consideration and guidance makes Raju think of his own problems.

All his problems and troubles generate from his first acquaintance with Rosie. Raju wonders why she calls herself Rosie. She is not a foreigner but an Indian in Indian dress. Raju has enough shrewdness to tickle her vanity by saying that as an orthodox dancer, she fosters the Indian cultural tradition. Not only does he assess the weakness in Rosie's character but sees through the vulnerable personality of her husband, whom he calls Marco, without bothering to know his name. The shape of the narrative in *The Guide* is such that before we hear the protagonist's confession, we're given a brief but incisive sketch of the three significant characters who constitute a kind of triangle (not the kind of love triangle we usually come across in Hardy's novels), and the contours of the plot. The plot of *The Guide* is more complex than the plot of any other tale of Narayan. It presents the formation and the break-down of a man-woman relationship and the way in which the characters involved in the relationship try to seek self-realization in the traditional Indian sense. Rosie's husband is a permanent tourist obsessed with the history of cave paintings. He comes to Malgudi to study the Mempi cave paintings. His wife doesn't share his interests. On the other hand, she likes dancing as she comes from a family traditionally dedicated to the Hindu temples as dancers. These temple dancers are viewed as public women. In this context, one is reminded of Rangi in *The Man-Eater of Malgudi*. Rosie's mother looks after her education. After obtaining a master's degree in Economics, she finds it difficult to decide about the next step in her career. It is through a matrimonial advertisement that she comes into contact with Marco and marries him, because of family pressure. This inter-caste marriage goes wrong from the start, because the husband is absorbed in the study of painting and art, and he seems to treat his wife not cruelly but indifferently. It never crosses his mind that his wife is educated and has tastes and aspirations of her own. Having noticed the rift between the wife and the husband and bewitched by the beauty of the wife, Raju exploits the situation and establishes a rapport with the wife. He takes her around Malgudi and always tries to impress on her his responsibility as the guide. He himself explains the situation:

I was accepted by Marco as a member of the family. From

guiding tourists I seemed to have come to a sort of concentrated guiding of a single family. Marco was just unpractical, an absolutely helpless man. All that he could do was to copy ancient things and write about them. His mind was completely in it. All practical affairs of life seemed impossible to him; such a simple matter as finding food or shelter or buying a railway ticket seemed to him a monumental job. Perhaps he married out of a desire to have someone care for his practical life, but unfortunately his choice was wrong—this girl herself was a dreamer if ever there was one. She would have greatly benefited by a husband who could care for her career; it was here that a handy man like me proved invaluable. I gave up nearly all my routine jobs in order to be of service to them. (100)

The above passage brings to a central focus the preoccupations of the characters and the socio-cultural framework in which they operate. Entertaining Rosie becomes the guide's sole professional activity. As he says, "The only reality in my life and consciousness was Rosie. All my mental powers were now turned to keep her within my reach, and keep her smiling all the time." (104) But he finds it difficult to understand the girl. He says, "She allowed me to make love to her, of course, but she was also beginning to show excessive consideration for her husband on the hill. In the midst of my caresses she would suddenly free herself and say, 'Tell Gaffur to bring the car. I want to go and see him'." (105) Later he finds the reason for her melancholy and vacillation: her losing all hope to activate her talent as a dancer. The following dialogue unmistakably suggests this:

She asked me one evening, point blank,
"Are you also like him?"
"In what way?"
"Do you also hate to see me dance?"
"Not at all. What makes you think so?"
"At one time you spoke like a big lover of art, but now you never give it a thought."

> It was true. I said something in excuse, clasped her hands in mine and swore earnestly, "I will do anything for you. I will give my life to see you dance. Tell me what to do. I will do it for you." (107)

Raju utilizes to the utmost her passion for dancing to alienate her from her husband. Having heard the whole story from Rosie, Marco takes a stubborn step and refuses to acknowledge her as his wife. He tells her, "you are here because I am not a ruffian. But you are not my wife. You are a woman who will go to bed with anyone that flatters your antics. That's all. I don't want to hear, but if you are going to be here, don't talk. That is all." (134) It is because her husband refuses to take her along with him that Rosie comes to Raju. Their intimacy and freedom irritates Raju's mother, who leaves him to his fate. Living like a married couple to all appearances, they manage to organize dance programmes in and outside Malgudi, which bring fame and fortune to Rosie, who rechristens herself Nalini.

As it always happens in Narayan's fictions, there is a sudden fluctuation in the fortunes of Raju. This happens as an unobtrusive plot device. Marco's photograph appears in the *Illustrated Weekly of Bombay*, which Nalini reads regularly. Along with the photograph, she sees a review of his book, which is extolled as "An epoch-making discovery in Indian cultural history." (117) She immediately draws the attention of Raju to it and orders his secretary to immediately place an order for the book. This makes Raju realize that he has made a mistake all through their relationship in ignoring the existence of Marco, who, in fact, sends Raju a copy of his book, *The Cultural History of South India*, in which he acknowledges his indebtedness to Raju for helping him in Malgudi. Having learnt this from Mani, Rosie demands from Raju the reason for concealing the book from her. When Raju tells her that the book was sent to him and not to her and that she is showing unexpected and unanticipated interest in her husband's work, she tells him, crying, "After all, after all, he is my husband." (179) When Raju tells her that she has forgotten when and how he left her, she says, "I do, and I deserve nothing less. Any other husband would have throttled me then and there. He tolerated my company for nearly a month, even after knowing what I had done." (179) This statement of Rosie suggests that her awareness of herself and her lack of judgment in assessing the true nature of the wife-husband relationship becomes increasingly acute and makes Raju physically uncomfortable and mentally uneasy. While in prison, he thinks that Marco deliberately lodged a complaint with the police that he was guilty of forgery. Even in prison he entertains a fond hope that Rosie will wait till he comes out of prison. But she tells him that she may go back to her husband, and feels confident that he will accept her if she stops dancing.

Raju's life after his release from prison involves him in a trap, largely because of his innate inability to avoid interference in the affairs of others. In the narrative sequence that dramatizes Raju as a *sadhu*, we are constantly reminded that he is aware of the new role he is playing. His transformation from a tourist guide to a spiritual guide is saturated with unobtrusive but subtle irony. His cryptic statements suggest that he is playing the role of a pontiff. He feels that "he was attaining the stature of a saint." (15) The words "grand," "grandeur," and their analogues are often used to suggest the kind of illusion in which he is engrossed. It assumes a concrete texture and shape when we learn that "He was hypnotized by his own voice." (42) But the reader is always kept aware of this illusion by the narrator. The villagers call him "Swamiji" and compare him to Mahatma Gandhi. In spite of his eagerness not to betray himself, he loses his nerve to act as a saint and do penance to please the god of rain. When an American correspondent interviews him, he says, "I am only doing what I have to do; that's all. My likes and dislikes do not count." (218) This suggests that Raju realizes that his role-playing makes him commit himself to a course of action not because he wants it but because of the structural compulsions that govern the role-playing.

From the foregoing analysis, we can see *The Guide* as a text with a complex of meanings. The most significant of this complex of meanings is the self and the roles it can play. Raju, the tourist guide, plays the role of a guide to a particular family. He helps Marco complete a scholarly work. He helps Rosie actualize her potentiality as an artist. He plays the role of a spiritual guide to a village community. We may say that he does not achieve any realization of the self in the various roles in which he appears. But we can't ignore the fact that his confession to Velan is more sincere than the roles in which we see him. One may here reverse the famous phrase of Mark Schorer, "Technique as Discovery," to "discovery as technique." In the narrative of *The Guide*, we find that Rosie, at various stages, narrates her story to Raju. This helps her clarify to the self what it is and what it seeks. She realizes that acquiring name, fame, and wealth as an artist is not an end in itself. The self has not only aspirations but duties as well. It is in the process of actualizing her aspirations as an artist that she discovers her obligations and duties. Raju helps her master the illusion, and, in the course of mastering it, discover the self. Raju himself, one may hazard a comment, discovers the self by passing through the illusion that he is serving in the first instance a family and in the last instance society at large. Commenting on the end of *The Guide*, K.R. Srinivasa Iyengar writes: "Does it really rain, or is it only Raju's optical delusion? Does he really die, or merely sink down in exhaustion? Has the lie really become the truth, or has it been merely exposed? We are free to conclude as we like; Narayan might say in Pirandellian fashion: 'Right you are, it you think so'!"[10] But in *The Guide* the movie, the audience behold not just signs of rain but a sharp shower, authenticating the villagers's implicit faith in Raju the saint. When Narayan narrated to Graham Greene the story of *The Guide*, and was not able to decide for himself "whether to leave my hero alive or dead at the end of the story, Graham was definite that he should die."[11] The main issue appears to be whether a narrative should have a formal closure or an open ending. Narayan is not interested in giving a formal closure, which would have made Raju a scapegoat, if not a martyr. True to the Indian tradition, his tales do not end with a catastrophic close. On the other hand, they end with the protagonist's realization that he or she is involved in an illusion and that illusion is slowly but steadily yielding place to the staple truth, that is, life in its normal flux. This appears to be in harmony with the critical thinking on the crucial question of the ending in the modern novel. Unlike the ending in a Victorian novel which concludes with a death or a marriage, most modern novels end inconclusively. As Malcolm Bradbury points out, "in a great novel an extended human experience works itself out in all its complexity. In the entire activity, then, there resides a decided openness and a spirit of humanism, which have come to see part of the form."[12] If Bradbury's observation is applied to the text under review, we can see that *The Guide* unfolds a very complex kind of human experience which hardly finds a definite and predetermined end. It is pre-eminently a comedy of the self, in the sense that the self has to pass through a process of learning and unlearning, and self-evaluation has its own pain and its own sweetness and light. Perhaps it is this quality in Narayan's fictions that makes them perennially significant without any loss of their contemporaneity.

The Man-Eater of Malgudi and *Mr. Sampath* have thematic and structural similarities. They dramatize the nature and the significance of evil, which Narayan states as follows:

> The strong man of evil continues to be reckless until he is destroyed by the tempo of his own misdeeds. Evil has in it, buried subtly, the infallible seeds of its own destruction. And however frightening a demon might seem, his doom is implied in his own evil propensities—a profoundly happy and sustaining philosophy which unfailingly appeals to our people, who never question, "How long, oh, how long, must we wait to see the downfall of evil?"[13]

The profoundly happy and sustaining philosophy which unfailingly appeals to our people is given a creative rendering in the two texts—*The Man-Eater of Malgudi* and *Mr. Sampath.* Most critics of Narayan have elaborately discussed the mythic scaffolding in the texts. But what is more significant than the mythic scaffolding is the realistic context and the swift action that characterize the texts. Moreover, they are good illustrations of the comic sense of life that inheres in Narayan's fictions. The protagonists of both the tales—Nataraj and Srinivas—come from families which we may call traditional. Each in his own way practises the ethic of altruism that any householder has to preach and practise. Nataraj has a press, but he appears to be indifferent to the financial aspects of his trade. A poet and a journalist are his close friends, and every evening they indulge in gossip of all kinds. It is in this circle of ineffective but harmless and well-meaning men that Vasu enters. By profession a taxi-dermist, Vasu comes to Malgudi to improve his trade and business by killing animals in the Mempi forest. Vasu seems to have a good academic background; and like many enthusiastic young men, he takes an active part in the civil disobedience movement against British rule and courts arrest and imprisonment. Without imbibing social and ethical values that participation in a great struggle like the civil disobedience movement ought to generate in a person with a good academic background, Vasu becomes the disciple of a *pahelwan*, who makes him physically strong and teaches him the art of twisting and smashing stones. He becomes very popular among the crowds for his physical feats, but his master takes the money without sharing it with him. This makes Vasu lose his temper and turn against his master. When he tells his story to Nataraj, Nataraj realizes that Vasu would always be ungrateful to people for the help he receives from them. Expounding his philosophy of human conduct, Vasu tells Nataraj, "Life is too short to have a word with everyone in this land of three hundred odd millions. One has to ignore most people."[14] When Vasu starts bullying his friends, Nataraj feels, "If I had cared for a peaceful existence, I should have rejected Vasu on the first day. Now it was like having a middle-aged man-eater in your office and home, with the same *uncertainties*, *possibilities*, and *potentialities*." (30, emphasis added) When Nataraj compares Vasu to a middle-aged man-eater, he seems to be aware of an exaggeration which is not devoid of truth. Nataraj is prepared to give the man-eater his due. Vasu takes him in his jeep to the Mempi forest but leaves him near a tea-stall when somebody brings the news that a tiger is roaming nearby. The tea-stall owner, Muthu, helps Nataraj reach Malgudi. Muthu tells Nataraj that Vasu is sometimes strict. Though he tells Muthu that Vasu is "A fearless man" (45) only in order to please him, he is aware that Vasu is really courageous. But the problem that Nataraj faces is to contain this fearless man, so that he may not be a menace to him and to society. Vasu not only abuses the hospitality of Nataraj but slowly transforms himself into a threat to entire society. For example, he needlessly shoots the pet dog of a neighboring family, which makes an old man of the family and his grandson tremble with fear and agony. Nataraj realizes that the comparison he made between a man-eater and Vasu is not just a metaphor but an actuality. Vasu's taxidermy is no doubt creative, but Vasu's is utterly diabolic. When Vasu pushes a stuffed eagle to the gaze of Nataraj, Nataraj is bewildered. He tells Vasu that an eagle is *garuda*, the vehicle and the messenger of the god Vishnu. Vasu immediately catches the idea and says:

> I think there is a good business proposition here. I can supply them stuffed eagles at about fifty rupees each. Everyone can keep a sacred *garuda* in the puja and I'll guarantee that it won't fly off. Thus they can save their eyes from glare. I want to be of service to our religious folk in my own way. (64)

It is not Vasu's activities but the way he looks, talks, and thinks that make Sastri call him a *rakshasa*. He mentions the names of various *rakshasas* like *Ravana, Mahisha* and *Bhasmasura*, who destroyed themselves in pursuit of their own destructive aims. But Nataraj tries to give a social and secular interpretation to the Vasu-phenomenon. Totally agreeing with Sastri's interpretation, Nataraj tells him, "Sastri, you know the old proverb, that when your cloth is caught in the thorns of a bush, you have to extricate yourself gently and little by little, otherwise you will never take the cloth whole?" (95)

The significance of this action-packed tale is to be explored not by stressing the importance of Vasu, a social evil, but in terms of the panic, hesitation, and resistance he generates in Malgudi, may be in society at large. The destruction of this social evil, which is otherwise labelled *asura*, or *rakshasa*, takes the form of a high comedy in which a disreputable woman, Rangi, a temple elephant called Kumar, and, curiously enough, a mosquito play a crucial role. But there is a subtle irony here. Though a disreputable woman, Rangi is a temple dancer. She can't tolerate the idea of killing an elephant that does service to God. She has the courage to reveal to Nataraj the secret plan of Vasu to shoot the elephant when it leads the procession which is a part of the temple festival. Vasu, though a giant, is afraid of a mosquito. Very early in the narrative, when Sastri removes all the waste-paper from the attic in the press, Vasu tells Nataraj, "That fellow has done you a service in carrying away all that waste paper, but he has dehoused a thousand mosquitoes—one thing I can't stand," and adds, "Night or day, I run when a mosquito is mentioned." (26) When the procession led by Kumar, the elephant, is on its way from the temple, Vasu prepares himself to shoot the elephant. When the police disturb him for interrogation, he loses his temper and breaks his cot-frame to exhibit his strength. Since the cot is damaged, he sits in a chair instead of sleeping on his cot protected by a mosquito-net. Though Rangi fans him to keep the mosquitoes away, she cannot do it for long. When she falls asleep with fatigue, the mosquitoes return. Vasu wakes up from his doze, and while boxing a mosquito on his forehead, he gives himself a fatal blow.

The Man-Eater of Malgudi may be taken as a fable, just as Golding's *Lord of the Flies* is considered a fable. Golding insulates his boys in order to dramatize their response to one of the greatest temptations, power. In *The Man-Eater of Malgudi*, Narayan places Vasu, the mythic *rakshasa*, in a realistic context. Vasus are not aliens in society; they are very much a part of it. Nataraj and his friends are placed in a serious situation by the presence of Vasu. He not only destroys life, but defiles society and subverts religion by making a pretence of doing religious service. While the problem is serious, the efforts of Nataraj and his friends to contain and eliminate Vasu appear comic. The narrative is a significant and relevant comment on the anti-social forces that operate within society, but the mode of narration is comic and entertaining.

The novel that resembles *The Man-Eater of Malgudi* in the Narayan canon is *Mr. Sampath (The Printer of Malgudi)*. The key episode in *Mr. Sampath* is the crazy act of Ravi, who knocks down Sampath, who plays the key role of Shiva in the film "The Burning of Kama." The crazy behaviour of Ravi, an amateur painter and the protege of Srinivas, is the result of his obsession that Shanti, who plays the role of Parvathi in the film, is the girl who haunts his dreams and makes him sleepless. The plot of *Mr. Sampath* is complex. Srinivas, the protagonist, starts his career as the editor of *The Banner* with the help and goodwill of Sampath, the proprietor of the Truth Printing Works. Yielding to the flattery of Sampath, Srinivas neglects his editorial work and writes the script for the film "The Burning of Kama." While writing the script, Srinivas is aware of the moral and the spiritual signification of the myth. When Rati, Manmata's wife, weeps and prays to Lord Shiva to restore her husband to her, he tells her, "He is not lost, he is bodyless, that is all; his grossness has been burnt up, but he lives in essence. I grant that his activities may continue, though unseen, and I also grant that he may stay about my presence, along with my other unseen, invisible attendants."[15] Srinivas's advice to Ravi, whose infatuation for his dream girl goes crazy, almost echoes Shiva's words to Rati. Srinivas tells Ravi, "Like Shiva, open your third eye and burn up Love, so that all its grossness and contrary elements are cleared away and only its essence remains: that is the way to attain peace, my boy."[16] As Srinivas explicates it, the myth signifies the burning of desire which leads to the generation of love. In other words, sex is not an end in itself but a means to an end. The secularization of the myth consists in transforming lust into love. Except Srinivas, all the other characters connected with the making of the film reveal and bring to the fore various kinds and degrees of lust. Mr. Sampath closes his press and tries to acquire money in various unapproved ways to finance the project. He takes money from Srinivas's landlord, telling him that he would secure a good alliance for his daughter. To satisfy Srinivas, he employs Ravi to paint a few pieces of scenery. He brings Shanti and tells Srinivas that she is distantly related to him. When the actor playing the role of Shiva refuses to co-operate with them, Sampath himself plays the role. Srinivas later realizes that Sampath doesn't go home after the work is over, that he has been neglecting his wife and children, and also that Shanti is not his cousin, and they belong to different castes. When he draws Sampath's attention to the misery and unhappiness of his wife, he says, "Some people say that every sane man needs two wives—a perfect one for the house and a perfect one outside for social life. . . . I have the one. Why not the other? I have confidence that I will keep both of them happy and if necessary in separate houses. Is a man's heart so narrow that it cannot accommodate more than one? I have married according to Vedic rites: let me have one according to the civil marriage law." (179) Sampath's reply to Srinivas unmistakably suggests the comic tone and the tempo of the narrative. As in the other novels of Narayan, in *Mr. Sampath* also, when the plot reaches its climax, there is a sudden twist, a shattering reversal, caused by Ravi's assault on Sampath when the shooting of a love scene between Shiva and Parvathi is in progress. It is as though Shiva opened his third eye and burnt all lust. Shanti swoons and Sampath stands dazed. The whole set goes ablaze, because of short circuit in the electric installation. Police arrive and normality is restored. Sampath brings home Ravi from police custody. Sampath leaves Malgudi and Srinivas returns to continue his work as the editor of *The Banner*. Some time later Sampath meets Srinivas, narrates his experiences with Shanti and assures him that he is still a monogamist, for the simple reason that Shanti left him when both of them were sleeping at the Koppal railway station waiting for the train bound for Madras. The comic implications of the narrative appear clear in the reply of Sampath to Srinivas's question "What is to happen to the film?" (218) Sampath says, "It must be dropped. We've been abandoned by both Shiva and Parvathi. And only Kama, the God of love, is left in the studio." (218)

Mr. Sampath, while exploiting the religious significance of the myth, tells a secular tale. Like Nataraj devising ways and means to contain Vasu, we find Srinivas struggling to harmonize diverse men and attitudes and to canalize them into a creative and civilized achievement. Sampath and Ravi are the two characters who show, by their thought and action, the subversive and self-alienating compulsions associated with lust in its unabashed manifestation. The entire orientation of Srinivas, on the other hand, is towards the effacement of ego and lust, so that peace may prevail both at home and outside. One may wonder why the novel is called *Mr. Sampath*, if Srinivas is the central consciousness. The answer appears to be that Srinivas is meaningful not by himself but because of his association with Mr. Sampath, the owner of the Truth Printing Works. Ironically enough, the Truth Printing Works is far removed from the truth, which is the foundation of the policy of the editor of *The Banner*. *The Banner* is revived and continued; the Truth Printing Works remains closed. Sampaths are transitory. They are the eruptions of a decomposing social malaise.

It is difficult to place Narayan's comedy in any one of the well known categories like the comedy of manners, the problem comedy, the dark comedy, or the farcical and the satirical. In most fictions of Narayan, all these comic strains are noticeable, but none of them constitutes the dominant mode. Because of the inadequacy of any genre to describe the inclusive and vital quality of Narayan's fiction, it may not be inappropriate to call it the comedy of the self. As we have discussed earlier, Narayan's fiction is so inclusive that no aspect of life is excluded from it. A doting father, a shopkeeper, a sign-board-painter, an ardent feminist, a dedicated family-planning enthusiast, a dancer, a player who finds himself at home in the varied roles demanded by social exigencies, a teacher who establishes visual and spiritual communion with his dead wife, and a tiger and a *sanyasi* who guides him and gives him spiritual orientation have a place in Narayan's comic world. Malgudi is not a place in which virtue is rewarded and vice is punished. On the other hand, it is a world in which individuals alienate themselves from their families (and sometimes reunions take place), vice and virtue co-exist, and everything is possible, sometimes because of divine dispensation and sometimes because of intense human struggle. *A Tiger for Malgudi* dramatizes the harmony that is possible and the self-awareness that could be visualized when the human and the animal worlds are viewed as a simultaneous order. In his Introduction to *A Tiger for Malgudi*, Narayan says:

> Man in his smugness never imagines for a moment that other creatures may also possess ego, values, outlook, and the ability to communicate, though they may be incapable of audible speech.[17]

The above passage suggests man's very narrow and limited view of the self, which needs reorientation towards a larger world-view *A Tiger for Malgudi* precisely achieves this by bringing into play a unique kind of sensibility in which fact and fiction are subtly fused. The tiger narrates his own story. One may wonder whether a tiger can narrate anything at all. As a fictional character, the tiger makes his consciousness so transparent that the reader not only sees the working of his consciousness, but participates in the working of that consciousness. These observations may be clarified by scrutinizing the following passage:

> They have shown me special consideration, by the grace of my Master, whom I may not see again. All the same, lying here on the cool floor, I madly hope that my Master might suddenly appear out of a crowd, open the door of my cage, and command, "Come out, let us go." Such is my dream. I keep scrutinizing faces, but all faces look dull and monotonous, none radiant like my Master's. Men, women, and children peer through the bars, and sometimes cry aloud, "Ah, see this tiger. What a ferocious beast!" and make crude noises to rouse me, fling a stone if the keeper is not looking, and move on to appreciate similarly the occupant of the next cage. You are not likely to understand that I am different from the tiger next door, that I possess a soul within this forbidding exterior. I think, analyse, judge, remember and do everything that you do, perhaps with greater subtlety and sense. I lack only the faculty of speech.
>
> But if you could read my thoughts, you would be welcome to come in and listen to the story of my life. At least, you could slip your arm through the bars and touch me and I will hold out my forepaw to greet you, after retracting my claws, of course. You are carried away by appearances—my claws and fangs and the glowing eyes frighten you no doubt. I don't blame you. I don't know why God has chosen to give us this fierce make-up, the same God who has created the parrot, the peacock, and the deer, which inspire poets and painters. I would not blame you for keeping your distance—I myself shuddered at my own reflection on the still surface of a pond while crouching for a drink of water, not when I was really a wild beast, but after I came under the influence of my Master

and learnt to question, "Who am I?" Don't laugh within yourself to hear me speak thus. I'll tell you about my Master presently. (11-12)

Here, the narrative self seems to converge on the second person. The first sentence of the second paragraph amply demonstrates the point. The second person is invited by the narrative voice to read his thoughts to listen to the story of his life. But the narrative voice is very much aware that it is unlikely to happen. He says, "I don't blame you. I don't know why God has chosen to give us this fierce make-up." The narrative voice becomes lucid and inviting when he repeats, "I would not blame you for keeping your distance—I myself shuddered at my own reflection on the still surface of a pond while crouching for a drink of water, not when I was really a wild beast but after I came under the influence of my Master and learnt to question, 'Who am I?' Don't laugh within yourself to hear me speak thus. I'll tell you about my Master presently." The image of the tiger reflected on the surface of a pond horrifies him because the Master has generated within him that kind of transformation which we may, for lack of a precise term, call awakening. It may not be impossible to notice a slight allegory in the predicament of the tiger. If the self could behold an image of itself even without experiencing the kind of awakening that a Master can generate, the image might be as horrifying as the image of a tiger. When the Master intervenes and guides the self, the self realizes how ugly and incredible it appears.

The foregoing discussion helps us clarify an important point: the narrative voice and the second person become the inside and the outside of the fictional scene, so that they together explore the nature and the quality of "the Master's grace." The narrative voice says, "Every creature in the jungle trembled when it sensed my approach. 'Let them tremble and understand who is the Master, Lord of this world,' I thought with pride." (13) The word "Master" not only acquires multiple significance as the narrative proceeds but creates a thematic base which steadily evolves into an articulation of the voice of the Master. When the weaker sections of the animal world show their humility before the tiger, crying, "Here comes our

Lord and Master. Keep his path clear,'' (14) it pleases him, but the second person, ironically enough, is very much aware that the path is not clear. This inference is corroborated when the narrative voice says, ''Among our jungle community, we had an understanding, which was an acknowledgement of my superiority, unquestioned, undisputed. My Master, when I mentioned it, explained that it was also true of human beings in various degrees and versions.'' (14) This suggests that after all the jungle community is not entirely different from the human community. When the narrative voice, reminiscing his life in the forest, feels guilty for his lack of restraint, the Master, who reads his mind, says that ''there is nothing wrong in it, and advises me not to curb it—it being also a part of my own life, indispensable and unshakable although I have come a long way from it.'' (15) The words ''explain,'' ''read,'' ''advise,'' and their analogues that punctuate the narrative indicate the various ways in which a Master can guide the self through the vicissitudes of life. The jungle and the world are given metaphoric orientation, in the sense that they symbolize unobtrusively the various ordeals that the self may face before it earns an awareness of itself. When the narrative voice recollects, in a flash-back, the way in which it was trapped in the jungle, he also remembers the way the Master interpreted it. He says, ''My Master, later in my life, has mentioned hell, describing the conditions that would give one a feel of it. Now, recollecting the day of my trapping and the journey onward, *I realize its meaning.*'' (43, emphasis added)

The career of the tiger as a circus animal and the various ways in which it receives training from Captain constitute the comedy which we usually come across in Narayan. Captain, who captures the tiger, calls his circus ''Creative Circus.'' The relationship between Captain and his wife, Rita, develops into a familial crisis. She usually does the trapeze. Her husband, while trying to introduce a few innovations into the item, creates a problem for her, and she refuses to do the act as he wants it. This is paralleled by another item in which the tiger, christened Raja, participates. He is made to share a cup of milk with a goat. One day, when Raja is going through the item, the gluttonous goat, lapping up the milk, appears so lovely that Raja is tempted to put his teeth to it. As the impulse and the temptation grow stronger, in a flash Raja nips off the goat's head, creating confusion and commotion in the auditorium. Thinking that it is not safe to exhibit him in the circus, Captain tries to use the animal in the film-world. Curiously enough, the tiger, Raja, attains the status of a film-artist. But inside him, there is the inherent and characteristic stubbornness and ferocity of a tiger. When he is performing a film item, he suddenly gives a stunning blow to Captain and attains freedom from her circus master. He roams in Malgudi without any restraint and enters a school building to have a sound nap. When he wakes up, he realizes the situation. The efforts of the citizens of Malgudi to evacuate the tiger from the school remind us of the efforts of Nataraj and his friends to evacuate Vasu from Malgudi. It is at this juncture that the tiger meets the Swamiji, his Master. The Master is also a Malgudi citizen. A photographer of Malgudi, who has the talent of not forgetting a face which he looks at through his lenses, remembers that the Swamiji participated in the Quit India movement, after Independence lived with his family in affluent circumstances, and one day, without telling anybody, vanished from Malgudi, abandoning his wife and children. The Swamiji takes the tiger to a sequestered place at the foot of the Mempi range and gives him the kind of knowledge that is necessary for achieving selfhood. The tiger witnesses the Swamiji's activities. He receives many visitors who place their innumerable problems before him. His wife also pays a visit to him and tries to re-establish her relationship with him as his wife. He tells his wife, "I have forgotten the meaning of many words. Please do not force me to talk so much about myself. Because of my sympathies and a real desire to help you, I have spoken. Otherwise I never revive the identity of the past in thought or word; it's dead and buried." (172) By burying his past, the Master achieves a complete anonymity. When his wife pleads that he has to return home, he tells her, "Listen attentively: My past does not exist for me, nor a future. I live for the moment, and that awareness is enough for me. To attain this state, I have gone through much hardship. I don't have to explain all that now. I have erased from my mind my name and identity and all that it implies. . . . I wish I could help you, as I managed to help Raja and calm his turbulent soul." (171-72)

The Master not only achieves peace—awareness of the moment—but helps the tiger calm his turbulent soul. When the Master realizes that the time for attaining his *samadhi* is near at hand, he makes suitable arrangements for Raja's stay in a zoo, and tells him, "No relationship, human or other, or association of any kind could last forever. Separation is the law of life right from the mother's womb. One has to accept it if one has to live in God's plans." (174) The Swamiji's advice to Raja is a lucid thematic statement of the comedy of the self we have analyzed in the foregoing pages. An earlier version of this we have in *The English Teacher*, Narayan's controversial novel. Just as what is ferocious and turbulent cannot be tamed and creatively harnessed by mechanical and rigid exercises, what is agonizing and heart-rending cannot be mitigated by self-pity. As the Swamiji says, "separation is the law of life right from the mother's womb." Loss of the near and dear, and the consequent sadness need not be taken as articulations of the tragic. Krishnan in *The English Teacher* tries to overcome the grief caused by his wife's death not by succumbing to it but by living with it. He reflects:

> Wife, child, brothers, parents, friends. . . . We come together only to go apart again. It is one continuous movement. They move away from us as we move away from them. The law of life can't be avoided. The law comes into operation the moment we detach ourselves from our mother's womb. All struggle and misery in life is due to our attempt to arrest this law or get away from it or in allowing ourselves to be hurt by it. The fact must be recognized. A profound unmitigated loneliness is the only truth of life. All else is false. My mother got away from her parents, my sisters from our house, I and my brother away from each other, my wife was torn away from me, my daughter is going away with my mother, my father has gone away from his father, my earliest friends—where are they? They scatter apart like the droplets of a waterspray. The law of life. No sense in battling against it.[18]

As William Walsh succinctly puts it, "The second part of *The English Teacher* knits smoothly together Krishnan's devotion to his young daughter and—it is hard to put it down in plain language—his efforts to recover his connection with his dead wife."[19] The persistent and pressing memories of their familial life pursue Krishnan and act like an auto-suggestion. They evoke the image of Susila, and make Krishnan say repeatedly, "Susila" and "my wife," which act like a hypnotic melody. In a trance, he beholds his wife and feels intensely: "The boundaries of our personalities suddenly dissolved. It was a moment of rare, immutable joy—a moment for which one feels grateful to Life and Death." (213) Although he establishes a direct and immediate personal contact with his dead wife through a medium, he seems to dispense with the medium ultimately, for the simple reason that Susila becomes an inseparable element of his consciousness. Moreover, a close scrutiny of the text seems to suggest that there is a doubling of consciousness in such a way that the consciousness of Susila and the consciousness of Krishnan can enter into a dialogue without impairing the unity of the narrative discourse. For all practical purposes, the agony created by physical separation does not disturb the familial harmony of Krishnan's household. The self doesn't withdraw from the network of socio-familial obligations. On the other hand, the self operates in such a way that it keeps its relationship with the family and society intact, and at the same time achieves moments of rare and immutable joy.

In Narayan's comedy of the self, the self doesn't suffer from any kind of alienation from the family and society. The family, sometimes the joint family, is the basic unit of Narayan's Malgudi tales. Most of the protagonists achieve not philosophical wisdom but the sovereign principle of flexibility by passing through the common experiences of life, which constitute the very stuff of comedy.

NOTES

1. R.K. Narayan, *Reluctant Guru* (New Delhi: Orient Paperbacks, 1974), pp. 9-10.
2. J.P. Stern, *On Realism,* p. 28.
3. R.K. Narayan, *Gods, Demons and Others* (Mysore: Indian Thought Publications, 1967), p. 4.
4. R.K. Narayan, *The Financial Expert* (Mysore: Indian Thought Publications, 1979), p. 110.
5. "In my beginning in my end. . . ." T.S. Eliot, "East Coker," *Four Quartets* (1944; rpt. London: Faber and Faber, 1959), pp. 23-32.
6. Robert Bernard Martin, "Notes Toward a Comic Fiction," *The Theory of the Novel: New Essays,* ed. John Halperin (New York: Oxford University Press, 1974), pp. 86-87.
7. R.K. Narayan, *The Vendor of Sweets* (Mysore: Indian Thought Publications, 1967), p. 98.
8. R.K. Narayan, *The Painter of Signs* (Mysore: Indian Thought Publications, 1977), p. 5.
9. R.K. Narayan, *The Guide* (Mysore: Indian Thought Publications, 1967), p. 180.
10. K.R. Srinivasa Iyengar, p. 378.
11. R.K. Narayan, *My Days* (Mysore: Indian Thought Publications, 1979), p. 168.
12. Malcolm Bradbury, *Possibilities: Essays on the State of the Novel* (London: Oxford University Press, 1973), p. 12.
13. R.K. Narayan, *Gods, Demons, and Others,* p. 5.
14. R.K. Narayan, *The Man-Eater of Malgudi* (Mysore: Indian Thought Publications, 1973), p. 29.
15. R.K. Narayan, *Gods, Demons, and Others,* p. 93.
16. R.K. Narayan, *Mr. Sampath* (Mysore: Indian Thought Publications, 1973), p. 103.
17. R.K. Narayan, *A Tiger for Malgudi* (Mysore: Indian Thought Publications, 1983), pp. 7-8.
18. R.K. Narayan, *The English Teacher* (Mysore: Indian Thought Publications, 1981), p. 203.
19. William Walsh, *R.K. Narayan: A Critical Appreciation,* p. 56.

Arun Joshi: Self as Labyrinth

Arun Joshi's fiction explores the self and brings to a central focus the way in which the self tries to assess its involvement in the alienation from the family and society. For example, Sindi Oberoi in *The Foreigner* says,

> I worked in New York for a few more weeks, just enough to finish the project I had started. As it had happened after Babu's death the laboratory provided me a sanctuary where I could forget my conflicts, at least at the conscious level. But in the inner recesses of my mind the trial went on. Each day the judges met and examined the witnesses. My parents, my uncle, my lovers, Babu and June, their parents, and finally myself, one by one all were called by the invisible judges and asked to give their evidence. Under normal conditions this would have been painful but after the shock of June's death it came as a great therapeutic process. I felt as if some indefatigable surgeon was cleaning up my soul with the sharp edge of his scalpel.[1]

The above passage may be taken as a thematic statement of Arun Joshi's fiction. The exploration of the self is like "a great therapeutic process." By narrating his own experiences, Sindi Oberoi tells us how June, Babu, Mr. Khemka, and his daughter, Sheila, contribute in their own way to his understanding and awareness of the problems of the self. What is more, the passage seems to convey many levels of awareness through which he passes. Mr. Khemka's son, Babu, dies in a car accident in Boston. Sindi knows at the conscious level that he did not cause it. But an inexplicable fear haunts him. Perhaps it is this fear that converts the inner recesses of his mind into a court, where he is tried. But the oppressive nature of the trial takes a different shape, because of the shock created by the death of June, who is engaged to Babu but continues her association with Sindi. The image of the "indefatigable surgeon," reminding us of Eliot's "wounded surgeon,"[2] concretizes the therapeutic process and disinfects the self. Sindi comes to India and meets Mr. Khemka, who offers him the post of a manager in his firm. Pursued by a tormenting sense of guilt and uncertainty, he feels, "I tried to understand why I was afraid. It was nothing physical. They couldn't put me in prison. I feared something much worse—the abominable hands groping and probing into my own soul, ripping dry scars open and dipping into old wounds." (50) The participles "groping," "probing," "ripping," and "dipping" suggest that evaluation of the self is a very painful process. Sindi seems to experience the reality of the process whenever he is alone. He tells us, "When I did go out I walked about the streets lost within myself unseeing and unheeding while the scalpel continued to move from chamber to chamber and tissue to tissue cutting out much that was rotting and disembowelling cells which had never been seen before. It was an awesome sight." (207) The words "chamber," "tissue," and "cells" suggest that the self is a sort of labyrinth, and to subject the self to groping and probing is to pass through a maze. Narrating his love-affair with Kathy, the painful consequence of his separation from her, and the sadness caused by the separation, he says, "Even after several years, somewhere in the *labyrinth* of my consciousness the wound still bled. I felt sad and perhaps showed it." (72, emphasis added)

The image of the labyrinth signifies the nature and the function of the self. In this context, we may also note that the word "labyrinth" and its analogues occur quite frequently in Joshi's texts. The core of Joshi's fictional theme consists in viewing the self as a labyrinth, and any kind of assessment that the self makes of itself is a therapeutic process. This thematic concern in relation to his other novels we shall elaborately discuss when we take up each novel for discussion. Suffice it to say here that *The Foreigner*, while developing the theme of the self/soul/labyrinth, brings to the fore the social framework within which the theme becomes meaningful.

Sindi Oberoi, the protagonist-narrator of *The Foreigner*, is not exactly a foreigner but a rootless person. The entire narrative emerges in a reminiscent form. Not only in this text, but in Joshi's fiction as a whole, reminiscence is the major fictional device. All his protagonists narrate their experiences and these are unified not in terms of sequence and logic but in terms of the experiencing consciousness. Social and human relations are meaningful within the scope and reach of the narrative personality. For example, Sindi tells us,

> Somebody had begotten me without a purpose and so far I had lived without a purpose, unless you could call the search for peace a purpose. Perhaps I felt like that because I was a foreigner in America. But then, what difference would it have made if I had lived in Kenya or India or any other place for that matter? It seemed to me that I would still be a foreigner. My foreignness lay within me and I couldn't leave myself behind wherever I went. I hadn't felt like that when my uncle was living. It wasn't that I loved him very much or anything—as a matter of fact we rarely exchanged letters—but the thought that he moved about in that small house on the outskirts of Nairobi gave me a feeling of having an anchor. After his death the security was destroyed. (65)

The above citation is not remarkable for anything extraordinary but is significant enough to suggest an obvious case of rootlessness. Not only here, but in various other significant spots of the narrative, the word "foreign" and its substantive forms occur so as to make the term not just a label but an inclusive metaphor that governs and controls the narrative. Wherever he is, Sindi is a foreigner. The "foreignness" is not something external but something which the protagonist feels within. In other words, Sindi feels alienated, and the alienation is something that affects the self and makes it sad and subdued. From Kenya he moves to England, and finally to Boston, where he meets Babu Rao Khemka. Hired by the Foreign Students Office to look after the new Indian students, Sindi shows, at least outwardly, his interest in India and the Indians who come to study in Boston. From the start, Babu appears to be erratic and indiscriminate in his views and statements. It is through Sindi that Babu comes into contact with June. When June tells him that Americans are not very congenial towards foreigners, Babu makes an irrelevant comment: "Indians are so underdeveloped as compared to them. Sometimes I wish I had been born in America. Not that I have anything against India but there is nothing to beat America." (97) Sindi feels that it is the naivete with which Babu talks about his own feelings that makes him very confusing, if not embarrassing. But, curiously enough, June likes Babu precisely for his unselfconscious expression of his feelings. As their intimacy develops, June finds it difficult to disentangle herself from Babu, but at the same time she finds it hard to dissociate herself from Sindi. Whether Sindi really loves her need not trouble us. When she asks him to marry her, he tells her, "I am not the right kind of man for you. Some people are not really cut out for marriage." (111) Sindi seems to have preconceived views about love. He broods over his relationship with Anna, Kathy, and June, and wonders whether he was in love with any one of them at any time. He tells June, "At least I have loved people as much as I love myself. It isn't much but that is not my fault. And then to be in love in your sense requires one to take things seriously, assume that there is a permanence about things. Nothing ever seems real to me, leave alone permanent. Nothing seems to be very important." (119) And hesitantly adds, "Good things and bad things appear to be the same in the long run of existence." (114) The word "existence" may compel us to conclude that Sindi is talking like an existentialist. But this may be a misleading inference in the total context of Sindi's rootless and alienated self. The process of discovering the self, as has been noted earlier, is a sort of cleansing and disinfecting exercise, and has a diagnostic implication. In understanding Babu's self-created problems, such as his failure in the examination, his obsession that he thinks a lot about women, his commitment to his home, and his nostalgic ravings, Sindi tries to clarify the problematic of the self. As he says, "For the first time in many years I found myself thinking of the future. I wondered how it was going to turn out. Once it would have turned out in just one way, but now it was pregnant with alternatives. And the choices I made now would inevitably lead me to one of the alternatives. And there was no getting away from what I had chosen so far. After years of struggle I had almost achieved what I had always wanted to be; without desire. But I had bartered away the gains in an attempt to possess a woman. I had exchanged the steady tranquillity of my being for the excruciating moments of ecstasy in a woman's body." (124) This confession of the protagonist stems from the fear that he may lose the company of June. It almost amounts to the self struggling to have and not to have attachment with the flux of life. This tantalizing situation is made more complicated by the sympathy June shows Babu. She writes to Sindi, "I have been seeing Babu frequently since you left. He seems to be in such low spirits most of the time that my heart aches for him. He is usually depressed because he is not doing very well in his studies. I go out with him every night because I think he needs me. I want to be of use to him. Perhaps, as you would say, it is all illusion: one can never be of use to any one. Perhaps I am being selfish. All I know is that I find a strange peace when I am soothing him. I do so much want to be of help to someone, Sindi. Without that life would seem so empty." (125) In this love-triangle, the victim appears to be June, whose system of preferences and priorities is meaningful within the framework of human values and human relations. Though she gets engaged to Babu, the wedding doesn't take place, because of Babu's obstinacy and his repeated failure in the university examinations. The situation becomes precarious when the university asks Babu to leave because he has repeatedly failed in the examinations. Moreover, June becomes pregnant, and Babu's taunting comments make her awfully unhappy. One day, in one of his irritable and nasty moods, he quarrels with June and leaves the flat, driving his car in a fit of rage and despair. He hits it to an overpass and dies in the accident. Sindi breaks the news of Babu's death to June and sends a message to his father in India. Sometime later, June has an abortion and dies. The complications created by his affair with June and his relationship with Babu, and their deaths cause an agonizing introspection in Sindi. As he puts it,

I was seized with the problem of once again putting together all that had happened to me and *coming to grips with life.* For twenty years I had moved whichever way life had led me. I had learnt much on the way. I had learnt to be detached from the world, but *not from myself.* That is when the fatal error was made that ultimately led to Babu's and then to June's death. (207, emphasis added)

The above crucial passage sums up the thematic concerns of *The Foreigner.* As we have noted earlier, a foreigner is not one who stays in a country not his own but one who suffers from a sense of rootlessness. This feeling inevitably leads to self-alienation. If the self is detached from the world, it may gain a certain amount of objectivity and human perspective. But this is not enough if the self is to earn the awareness that would clarify the objectivity further and make it a mirror in which images of society could be reflected.

Sindi comes to India and, as the manager of Khemka's firms, gets closer to Babu's sister, Sheila. It is by constantly talking to Sheila about Babu and by close-reading Babu's correspondence with his sister that Sindi discovers the disastrous consequences of alienating the self from its roots. It is Sheila's solemn and controlled sadness, now and then coming to the fore during their conversations, that makes Sindi gain the human perspective and understand the meaning of familial relationship in the Indian context. The following dialogue amply demonstrates the insight that Sindi gains:

"Your father is a selfish old man and now the laws of existence are bringing his avarice home to him. Who are you or I to stand in the way? He must suffer if he wants to stop being a jackal and become humane."

Suddenly Sheila broke in, quietly but decisively.

"Would you stop calling him a jackal? Your may be a wise man and I might admire you for your wisdom. But you forget how long it has taken you to get where you are. And all the destruction that you have caused in the process."

She was right and I had nothing to say. (230-31)

Arun Joshi's protagonists are highly idiosyncratic characters. The usual fictional themes we find in the Indian novel in English—for example, the theme of identity, the East-West encounter, the rural India—do not appear in Joshi. Brooding and retrospective, Joshi's protagonists struggle to overreach the self. Sindi Oberoi, Kenya-born Indian of doubtful parentage, gets a doctoral degree in mechanical engineering from an American university, but his technical virtuosity recedes to the background when he gets bogged down in a mess of human relations. Billy (Bimal) Biswas, a US-trained anthropologist, tries to harmonize his scholarly and human concerns but seems to fail to achieve an integration, largely because of the social hostility his actions create. The narrator of *The Strange Case of Billy Biswas*, at the outset of the narrative, says:

> Looking back . . . it is not so much the final resolution of his life that interests me as I am intrigued by what preyed upon him during the course of it. If life's meaning lies not in the glossy surfaces of our pretensions but in those *dark mossy labyrinths of the soul* that languish forever, hidden from the dazzling light of the sun, then I do not know of any man who sought it more doggedly and, having received a signal, abandoned himself so recklessly to its call. In brief, I know of no other man who so desperately pursued the tenuous thread of existence to its bitter end, no matter what trails of glory or shattered hearts he left behind in his turbulent wake.[3] (Emphasis added)

The narrator seems to suggest that life's meaning doesn't lie in the world outside but within. The "glossy surfaces" are contrasted with the "dark mossy labyrinths of the soul." This unmistakably suggests that the soul/self has innumerable chambers whose significance can't be unravelled. If one tries to pursue this kind of enquiry "doggedly," society considers him strange and a useful case for a psychiatrist. The narrator meets Billy Biswas in New York, where he is studying anthropology. Though he comes from the upper stratum of Indian society, Billy lives in Harlem because he feels that white America is much too civilized for him. Even in America, he keeps himself aloof and has only a few friends. He returns to India to teach anthropology in Delhi University. He marries Meena Chatterjee, but their familial relationship goes wrong from the beginning. Billy's preoccupations are such that he travels extensively and comes up with certain social facts that are not normal. For example, when Billy, his father, and the narrator discuss a murder, Billy says, "The point, however, is this: Is it possible for an ordinary person—a government clerk, let us say—to receive a message from a goddess and, having received one, to pass into another world, not for an hour or a day but for a week, a month, one whole year, at the end of which he may return to his normal state. If this happens, as it seems to have happened in this case, what is to be the attitude of the society, of the law, if you please?" (53) Billy seems to be aware of the hostile attitude of society to any event which has supernatural and occult implications. When his father disapproves of his theory, Billy tells him, "It is only after it happens to oneself that one comes to believe. But, I am afraid, we have got side-tracked. I don't personally care whether the son got well because of the sacrifice or without it. All I am saying is that *there are worlds at the periphery of this one, above it and below it, and around it, of which we know nothing until we are in them.*" (54-55, emphasis added) Billy's father conducts a trial in which a clerk is accused of sacrificing a boy to propitiate the goddess Kali in order that the clerk's young son, suffering from leukemia, should get well. We are not concerned with the problem of justice the case brings to the fore; we are interested in Billy's response. The passage just cited amply demonstrates Billy's interest in and fascination for unusual psychic phenomena. His investigations as an anthropologist confirm his intuitions as a man and explain why his wife is not happy with him.

One fine morning he disappears, and even the C.I.D. investigations fail to trace his whereabouts. One of his girl friends, Rima Kaul, who loved him passionately, meets the narrator two years after Billy's disappearance and requests that the strange case of Billy Biswas be reopened. The narrator, who is also the Collector of Jhansi District, thinks that it would be a futile exercise. But after reading the correspondence between Tuula and Billy sent for his perusal, he realizes that Billy's whereabouts may be traced. In one of his letters, Billy says, "It seems, my dear Tuula, that we are swiftly losing what is known as one's grip on life. Why else this constant blurring of reality? Who am I? Who are my parents? My wife? My child? At times I look at them, sitting at the dinner table, and for a passing moment I cannot decide who they are or what accident of Creation has brought us together." (97) The self-questioning that is noticeable in this passage is caused by Billy's dreams, in which he sees a strange woman who appears to be both familiar and unfamiliar. The narrator learns the significance of Billy's dreams and his psychic disturbance from Billy himself, when he visits a hamlet ravaged by a terrible drought. Billy appears in rags, and, after exchanging formal courtesies, narrates his experiences since his disappearance from Delhi. In one of his expeditions to the rural areas in central India, when he was asleep, he had a dream so erotic that it upset him. Pressurized by the psychic trouble and an inexplicable erotic compulsion, he sat under a *saal* tree and gazed at Bilasia dancing. Bilasia was a rural girl, whose face Billy could identify as that of his dream-girl. Though he encountered a number of obstacles, he succeeded in marrying the village girl. Though he lives at the subsistence level, he is happy. He tells the narrator, "What kept us happy, I suppose, were the same things that have kept all primitives happy through the ages: the earth, the forest, the rainbows, the liquor from the *mahua*, an occasional feast, a lot of dancing and love-making, and, more than anything else, no ambition, none at all." (148)

The narrator doesn't want to reveal Billy's whereabouts to his family, but social compulsions make him reveal the secret. The Biswas family get into action in order to claim Billy not only for the family but for the civilized society. They don't succeed, because in pursuing Billy the guards are compelled to shoot him in sheer self-defence. As the narrator concludes:

> The strange case of Billy Biswas had at last been disposed of. It had been disposed of in the only manner that a humdrum society knows of disposing its rebels, its seers, its true lovers.

> Sitting there, watching the shades of evening settle slowly on the drab little town, it seemed to me that nothing but blind blundering vengeance, howsoever camouflaged, awaits all those who dare to step out of its stifling confines. It is a confrontation whose outcome is as certain as the end of solitary boats beating against a maelstrom.
>
> It is unlikely that Billy was unaware of all this when that torrid afternoon he for the first time stepped out of the sanctuary of the great god of the primitive world who had until then guarded him as his own. It was also unlikely that he was not aware of the impossibility, in the world that he had abandoned, of saving men from themselves. It was this, more than anything else, that, for me, made his end so unbearably tragic. (240-41)

The foregoing comments of the narrator suggest that Billy is aware of the hurdles he has to face when he leaves the primitive world to re-enter the world of civilization. We gather from the narrator's comments that Billy is more sensitive to certain experiences than to others. His affair with Rima Kaul and his marriage with a tribal girl obliquely suggest that he is prepared to take a great risk in order to test the validity of some of his intuitions about life. After his re-entry into the civilized world, he tells the narrator:

> Any choice worth its name is drastic. It is another matter that we whistle it down or gloss over it until it ceases to be drastic. At the same time it ceases to be meaningful, either. Sometimes I think the human mind is equipped with built-in apparatus for compromises. As soon as you are faced with a difficult choice this apparatus is switched on. It runs about here and there, brokering between various parts of man, rationalizing this, postponing that, until what is left is the conventional expedients of the age and hardly a choice. Deep down we are afraid that the price of making such choices is terrible, not realizing that the price of not making them is even more terrible. (190)

The passage brings to a central focus the thematic complex of Joshi's fiction. The self/soul/labyrinth is placed at the crossroads where the conscious and the unconscious impulses meet. This, we can say, is a crisis which involved the self in personal and metaphysical dilemmas of existence. In Billy's opinion, the built-in apparatus for compromises with which the human mind is equipped inclines towards conventional expedients of the age, thereby suggesting the self's impotence to choose what is right. Billy calls this corruption, and adds, "What could be more terrible than corruption." (190) *The Apprentice* elaborates the theme of corruption of the self in a society which is itself corrupt. Himmat Singh tells Ratan Rathor, "My soul was killed, you put yours to pawn. But souls that were pawned could perhaps be retrieved. . . . May be souls are like muscles, Ratan Rathor. May be to develop them one has first to put them to use."[4] The word "muscles" calls to mind the passage in *The Foreigner* in which Sindi confesses: "When I did go out I walked about the streets lost within myself unseeing and unheeding while the scalpel continued to move from chamber to chamber and tissue to tissue cutting out much that was rotting and disembowelling cells which had never been seen before. It was an awesome sight." (207) The process of retrieving souls is an "awesome" process, and Joshi makes use of "labyrinth" and its analogues to graph it.

The Apprentice is a fictional experiment—a confessional novel which employs psycho-narration. Ratan Rathor narrates the way in which he became a victim of corruption in a metropolitan society during the war between India and China. His audience is a student, who just listens; the narrator himself puts the questions and expresses the doubts that may arise in the listener's mind. The narrative runs like a monologue of Browning, in which there is an audience whose participation is just passive. The son of a freedom fighter who laid down his life for the sake of a cause, Ratan Rathor comes to Delhi during the later stages of the Second World War in search of a job. Through the good offices of a stenographer, he is appointed a temporary clerk in a department for war purchases. His first boss, the Superintendent, noticing his docility and implicit obedience, recommends him for confirmation. After his confirmation, Rathor becomes a careerist. He shamelessly pursues advancement in his career and agrees to marry the Superintendent's niece. Though all his colleagues call him a whore, he turns a deaf ear to their sarcastic comments and concentrates on getting ahead of others in pursuit of his ambition. As an officer in the military stores department, he clears spurious war material after taking a bribe from Himmat Singh, a notorious character. He has a friend, the Brigadier, who absconds from the front when the Indian army is suffering reversal and humiliation at the hands of the Chinese. After the ceasefire, the military authorities suspect that a shady deal was responsible for sending useless war material to the front. Not only has it caused loss of life and disaster, but it also humiliates the country. Ratan Rathor is very much aware of this. The intelligence branch of the army suspects Ratan Rathor and authorizes an S.P. to interrogate him in a prison cell. But Himmat Singh, using his influence, gets Ratan Rathor released from police custody. Meanwhile another serious situation develops. The military authorities institute a court-martial to try Ratan Rathor's friend, the Brigadier, for deserting the army. The S.P. once again contacts Rathor and tells him that if he confesses his guilt, it may help the Brigadier escape court-martial. When he makes a decision to confess, Rathor learns that the Brigadier has killed himself. Immediately Rathor goes to Himmat Singh in order to wreak vengeance, but Himmat Singh tells him that the Secretary has double-crossed him. He takes him to the Secretary but by then Rathor's determination to wreak vengeance on his betrayers loses its hold on him.

The above summary of the novel demonstrates the kind of society in which Ratan Rathor lives and pursues his ambition. The narrative is punctuated with words like "sham," "bogus," "whore," "humiliation," "fake," and other similar words. Rathor's father calls career-making "bourgeois filth." (33) The word "filth" occurs too often to go unnoticed. For example, Himmat Singh "was born in filth and in filth he had grown." (144) There is a close correspondence between the pursuit of career-making we notice in Ratan Rathor and in Himmat Singh. Starting his career as a shoe-shine boy, Himmat Singh becomes a pimp, a petty thief, a waiter, and finally involves himself in a minor black market racket. As the narrator puts it, "With the success of his rackets he was now face to face with the men who had had his foot broken, who had, perhaps, made a whore of his mother. Those men had angered him. And then they had made him laugh. . . . He had taken first to women, then to drink, and finally to drugs." (145) The ubiquitous nature of corruption is such that not only persons like Himmat Singh, Rathor, the Secretary, and the Minister, but the *pujari* in the temple which Ratan Rathor frequents is also not free from it. When his son's payment is stopped, he approaches Rathor for help. The *pujari*'s son is a contractor and builds three hundred quarters for slum-dwellers in a record time. The new engineer refuses to pass the bills because he notices too much sand in the mortar. Even though Rathor tells him that his department is different, the *pujari* persists in his request, and as Rathor puts it, "He said he would not mind if he spent some money to get all that done. Everyone had the right to a cut. He said he understood that. He could suitably meet the desires of all concerned, the clerks, the officers, of the engineer concerned, even, here he asked me to forgive his impudence, even mine. MINE. MINE. He said he was a poor man and could hardly afford bribes but he did not mind it in a case like that. After all, he said, we all had to live. And that boy was his only son. He said he would give me any reasonable cut that I demanded." (124) The *pujari*'s problem and the means he employs to solve it characterize a society in which all values are inseparably tied to the craft of making money. As it usually happens, the more the money, the greater the frustration that accompanies it. The narrator, in spite of his awareness, fails to get out of the corruption racket. He finds his daughter and his wife always showing some sort of discontent. Even though he doesn't need money, he takes a bribe. As he reflects,

> First of all, I did not need the money. I am quite sure of that. I needed it no more than sitting here, after two cups of tea, I need a third. I may drink it because others do, or because it is offered free, but I need it for neither survival nor happiness. In this poor land I can be called comfortable, even well-off. I have a car, a flat, a concrete roof, running water. I have a refrigerator. My wife is not swimming in sarees but she does

not even use what she has. My daughter has all the money she needs; for college, clothes, and the cinema. We eat as much as a human being can possibly eat. Our health is looked after by the government. There are delays no doubt but with a bit of telephoning—I have a telephone which is not common—one always gets it. I have insurance. I have twenty thousand in the bank which is not a fortune but will tide you over a rainy day. Besides, I would have pension when I retire which should be enough for me and my wife. My daughter, God willing, should be married by then.

> So, you see, I did not need the money. If I had ever needed money it was when I had been offered it the first time—by the contractor—and I had refused. (61)

The passage, while revealing the tormenting and tortuous self-examination of the self when it is sorting out its own problems, unmistakably suggests some of the civilized values that obtain in a metropolis. The self-analysis makes the narrator discover that along with money one involves oneself in other new distractions like women and power, and becomes crazy about "brand-new enjoyment." (78) As he reflects, "I was expected to behave. Instead, I had merely walked into a brothel hounded by a strange disturbance. All that I could think of was my money and the fact that I was not enjoying life or what I imagined enjoying life meant. The more money I accumulated, the more I was dissatisfied and the more I was determined to 'enjoy' life. And all the time I thought of *death.*" (89, emphasis added) The word "death" obliquely suggests that a distracted life is death of the self. This may look like a philosophical commonplace, but a close look at *The Apprentice* reveals that there are ways of coming out of death, or what the narrator calls "the crookedness of the world; the crookedness of oneself." (148) As we have noticed earlier, retrieving souls that are pawned is an awesome process. The narrator-protagonist becomes an apprentice in order to learn the method of retrieving his own soul. Without entering the temple, he wipes the shoes of the congregation. He tells himself, "Be good. Be decent. Be of use. Then I beg forgiveness. Of a large host: my father, my mother, the Brigadier, the unknown dead of the war, of those whom I harmed, with deliberation and with cunning, of all those who have been the victim of my cleverness, those whom I could have helped and did not." (148-49) The process of activating the self in this solemn mood of penitence and expiation (which we noticed in the protagonist of *The Foreigner,* Sindi Oberoi) is amplified and given a symbolic resonance in *The Strange Case of Billy Biswas* and in *The Apprentice.* In *The Last Labyrinth,* this is very convincingly dramatized in Anuradha's decision to give up her relationship with Som Bhaskar.

In all his novels, Joshi employs first-person narration, which is disapproved of by Henry James, the champion of the "well-made novel." As Percy Lubbock, a Jamesian theorist, says, "It is very useful for enhancing the value of a picture, where none but the pictorial method is available, where we are bound to rely upon an intervening story-teller in some guise or other; it is much more satisfactory to know who the story-teller is, and to see him as a part of the story, than to be deflected away from the book by the author, an arbitrary, unmeasurable, unappraisable factor. But when the man in the book is expected to make a picture of himself, a searching and elaborate portrait, *then the limit of his capacity is touched and passed;* or rather there is a better method, one of finer capacity, then ready to the author's hand, and *there is no reason to be content with the hero's mere report.*" (Emphasis added)[5] A significant point that Lubbock makes in the above citation is that in telling his own story within the framework and conventions of realism, the hero or the protagonist cannot cover himself. In the three novels of Joshi we have just discussed, the first-person narration has restricted the meaning and the scope of the hero's role, thereby curtailing the significance of the novel as a whole. In *The Last Labyrinth,* Joshi seems to find a solution to this creative problem. He employs symbols well-known in Western literature, and invests new meanings on those symbols. As Gabriel Josipovici writes, "From the cunning passages, contrived corridors and issues of 'Gerontion,' through the mazes of Kafka, Proust, Beckett, Borges and Robbe-Grillet, the labyrinth has been the favourite image of modern literature."[6] The Cretan myth of the labyrinth and the Minotaur has been creatively used and variously interpreted by the writers mentioned in the above citation. The traditional reading of the myth brings out the worth of man as a hero and a quester. Borges in his story "The House of Asterion" deglamorizes the hero's triumph. Borges's story emphasizes the essential loneliness of man, and the pitiable nature of his existence and the brittleness of all speculative instruments that analyse it. The profound implications of the tale are suggested in what Theseus tells Ariadne, "The Minotaur scarcely defended himself."[7] It looks as though the relevance of the Cretan myth to our own time consists in the Minotaur's awareness of his loneliness and alienation and not in the triumph of Theseus. The Borgesian reorientation of the myth is relevant to our understanding of Joshi's *The Last Labyrinth*. The theme of alienation and loneliness in *The Last Labyrinth* is repeatedly suggested by the frequent use of the word "void." For example, Som Bhaskar, crossing the Manikarnika ghat, reflects,

> And here, on Manikarnika, were voids with a bang. Both within and without. That was probably how it had always been except that I had been too cocky to notice. You have to have a little "incident" or get a telephone at midnight about so and so popping off or catch your wife with another man or be told you have cancer to see the voids within. It was the voids and not the guava groves that I had walked through that morning my mother died; and voids too in her room in Bombay; and voids each time an affair ended; and the morning my daughter was born, and on and on. Voids all.[8]

The above passage brings into the fold of "void" birth, copulation, and death. It is at the root of Som's obsessive cry, "I want, I want, I want." The following dialogue between Leela Sabnis and Som repeats the point:

> "I am not fond of you," she told me one evening. "That would be lying, but I am concerned, I am worried. Tell me, what makes you tick?"
>
> "The voids," I said without enthusiasm.
>
> "The voids? What voids?"

"I hear this song way up in the sky. All the time."
"What song?"
"I want; I want; I want."
"I want. I want. I want. Just like that ?"
"Yes." (78)

Like the other protagonists of Joshi, Som Bhaskar seems to suffer from an excessive and unwarranted introspection. In one of his introspective moods he picks up the image, and the passage has a diagnostic implication:

> I had failed to make Geeta happy, or be anything more than a stranger to my children. My friends thought me a nut. I had been neglecting my companies. I had not even got over my mother's death. Or my father's, or the oppressive turbulence of the voids that never let me alone. Then, there was the greatest sorrow of them all—that no one even guessed: There was the sorrow of idleness. (109)

Leela Sabnis's psycho-analysis, the various psychiatrists he consults, and his doctor-friend, Kashyap, cannot help Som fill the voids in his existence.

The specificity and the evocative brilliance of the void image are comparable to the Borgesian story mentioned earlier in this discussion. But Joshi uses "labyrinth" as a metaphor that signifies soul/self not only in this novel but in his other novels also. In *The Last Labyrinth*, it appears as a creative comment on the void image. Som's "voids," obsessions and fornications impinge on Aftab Rai, Anuradha, and their residence, Lal Haveli, in Benaras. When he visits Aftab Rai's residence for the first time, Aftab tells him that "It is all run down now, this haveli, but its labyrinth remains." (35) When Som asks Aftab, "And what is in the last labyrinth?" he says, "Why, death, of course." (37) Death appears to be the dominating motif in the text and recurs in crucial contexts. Som Bhaskar seems to sink in the voids within and make a desperate attempt to disentangle himself from the voids without. His consciousness, in its attempt to over-reach itself for a total explanation of the void, gets stuck in the labyrinth which Aftab, Anuradha, and Gargi find meaningful in terms of their private vision. The death motif is amplified in the text so as to make it converge on the labyrinth image, as, for example, in the following passage:

> Was this maroon Blue Room a part of the labyrinth, too? If so, what was I doing here amidst these strangers? If someone, man or god, had watched my life from a great height, would I have appeared to him like an ant threading through a maze, knocking about, against one wall, then another? Were there spirits buried in these walls, deep down in forlorn dungeons? My mother believed in spirits. So probably did these people. If only one knew! If only miracles were to take place, as of old, and one could suddenly, irrefutably, know. Without nagging, enervating doubts. I want. I want. If only one knew what one wanted. Or, maybe, *to know* was what I wanted. To know. Just that. No more. No less. This, then, was a labyrinth, too, this going forward and backward and sideways of the mind. I felt again the faint stirrings of a curiosity that I had first felt near the marble sarcophagus, a secret curiosity that I dare not share with another. (53)

In the passage, the central images of the novel are subtly brought together. Som Bhaskar's cry, "I want, I want," points to the "void" in the background. The image "an ant threading through a maze" and the word "miracles" bring the "labyrinth" to the foreground. The miracle is associated with Gargi, who is a deaf-mute. But she communicates through signs, gestures, and writing. The daughter of a *Sufi Pir,* she is a devotee of Lord Krishna and worships *Srichakra.* We learn that her father gave Aftab his eyesight. Her grandfather had promised God his life if God spared his son's life; the son lived and the father died. Anuradha gives up Som in order to make Gargi give him a new lease of life. Som's escape from certain death caused by a stroke is indeed a miracle. His wife, Geeta, and his physician, Dr. Kashyap, are aware of it. Dr. Kashyap and Som go to the hill-temple to receive Aftab's shares from Lord Krishna (that is, from the temple authorities). Kashyap tells Gargi,

"I am a medical doctor. I do not believe in things in which Anuradha believes. But I know for a fact that Som had no chance whatsoever and I want to know: Did you save him? Anuradha says you did. And in return for what you did, she says, you made her promise that she would give up Som. For ever. That to her, Som would be dead, either way. Is this true? Please tell me." (206) But Gargi refuses to give any positive reply.

From the foregoing analysis, it follows that Som's "voids" are not unreal. He seems to comprehend life only in terms of alienation, aridity of feeling, and a sense of inner frustration. The persistent cry in the void appears to be "I want," which is juxtaposed with the whisper "I give," which constantly echoes in the labyrinth. This *discordia concors* can be clarified by analyzing the character of Anuradha.

Anuradha is the daughter of a disreputable woman, who was killed by one of her desperate lovers with a broken whiskey bottle. Anuradha, an orphan, grows up under the guardianship of her aunt in Bombay. Her original name is Meera. The name is very significant, because of the various visual and aural images of Krishna that proliferate through the text. Rechristened Anuradha, she spends some time in the film-world and gets out of it with the help of Aftab Rai, who introduces her to Gargi. She meets Som Bhaskar in one of the meetings of the shareholders connected with the production of plastic goods. Even in their first meeting she fascinates Som, and he is prepared to lose anything to retain her love. Whatever her antecedents may be, Anuradha is a labyrinthine woman, at once young and old, ancient and modern, and furious in lust and divine in love. She is every man's woman and no man's wife. She tells Som, "I can imagine I am married to Aftab. I can imagine I am married to you. My mother used to imagine she was married to Krishna." (128) We may add that she is also married to Krishna. In Joshi's text, the labyrinth earns the status of a metaphor for the various levels of consciousness immanent in the Krishna legend. As Som Bhaskar puts it, "There was nothing simple about Krishna. Had it been so, He would not have survived ten thousand years. He would have died along with the gods of the Pharaohs, the Sumerians, the Incas. Krishna was about as simple as the labyrinths of

Aftab's Haveli." (173) Som Bhaskar's vengeful pursuit of Aftab's shares takes him to the hill-temple where Gargi lives. What he sees there—for example, an old man making a hard journey along with his grandson to breathe his last in full awareness of entering the realm of death—makes him think of his question to Aftab and Aftab's answer:

> "And what is in the last labyrinth?"
> "In the last labyrinth?"
> "Yes."
> "Why, death, of course."
> I looked at him, puzzled.
> "I meant the labyrinth of this house." (37)

As we noted earlier, in discussing *The Apprentice*, the self, in shaping and learning the art of retrieving itself from voids, may sometimes enter a labyrinth, which is a metaphor for itself. In Joshi's novels, the juxtaposition of the void and the labyrinth images seems to suggest that there are two significant ways of making sense of life and the self. Life is not meaningful without the self's involvement in the family and society. As we have seen in Borges's retelling of the Cretan myth, there is a shift in the meaning and the perspective of the myth. The Minotaur is not a monster imprisoned in a labyrinth. He seems to suggest the theme of alienation and the encumbered self that has lost its moorings ever since the death of God. In Joshi's novels, this is signified by the void image. As Billy Biswas puts it, "Any choice worth its name is drastic," (190) and leads to a labyrinth. "Conventional expedients of the age" (190) lead to a void. Labyrinths are meaningful and make sense of life. They offer a total explanation for life and flux. Voids and wastelands are at best only half truths. The labyrinth as a metaphor for the various levels of awareness the self can attain is not without the echoes of Mino's legend. The Minotaur that one has to face in life's labyrinth is ultimately the self, may be the naked self. Leela Sabnis, in spite of her adherence to Descartes's *Cogito ergo sum*, keeps the two worlds—the world of matter and the world of spirit—separate. As Som puts it, "In the world of matter we had fed on sex and now we were satiated. In the world of spirit we still enjoyed conversation. The two worlds, by her lights, did not meet, could not meet." (81-82) While Leela Sabnis, a student of philosophy, fails to make sense of life and fails to make Som's life meaningful, a fusion of matter and spirit, Anuradha achieves it and saves Som from certain death.

Arun Joshi's themes have contemporary relevance and socio-cultural significance. *The Apprentice*, for example, is a creative comment on the crisis of character with which we have been familiar for a long time. But what we should not forget in reading the novel is its claim to be considered a novel, not a sociological study of the roots and causes of corruption. This observation applies with equal force to the other novels as well. *The Strange Case of Billy Biswas* is not about the manners and customs of the primitive tribes in Jhansi District but about Billy's sensitive response to certain unusual psychic phenomena and his whole-hearted pursuit of the meaning behind them. The narrator finds it difficult to convince his father and his wife that Billy's desertion of the family and society was propelled by some incoherent spiritual pursuit. They feel that "Billy had probably done something undesirable on a momentary impulse (I think she had something sexual in mind), something even more degrading than his affair with Rima Kaul, and did not have the courage to face his family. He might even have done it under duress. All along he had wanted to go back to them but was not sure how he would be received." (206) But the narrator and the reader know the psychic compulsion behind the leap of Biswas into an unknown and nebulous terrain. Explaining to the narrator the peculiar situation, Billy says, "It was as though a master mind had arranged the whole thing to give me a preview of what awaited me if I continued to defy its call. Poor Rima had crystallized for me the alternatives, although I did not realize this until I sat outside my tent that fateful night. I had two clear choices: I could either follow this call, this vision, whatever the cost, or be condemned to total decay. I suppose most men are faced with similar questions sometime or the other." (189-90) As we have noticed earlier, the choice to make a leap so that the self may be retrieved from decay is brilliantly exemplified in Anuradha in *The Last*

Labyrinth, when she takes the painful decision of snapping her links with Som Bhaskar so that he may live. These crucial decisions may plunge the self into an unknown terrain where the self, the family and society acquire new meaning. The new meaning emerges as a therapeutic process, a sort of cleansing. The self becomes an apprentice to itself, so that it may explore the labyrinth which is itself. As Ratan Rathor frankly confesses, "Then there is another thing that my father used to say, something in fact that *his* father had told him. Remember, he would say, whatever you do touches someone somewhere." (149) In fine, Arun Joshi's novels dramatize the truth embodied in Rathor's confession by forging an aesthetic pattern in which we come across dreams, stories within stories, characters experiencing hallucinations, and visions verbalized and reconstructed.

NOTES

1. Arun Joshi, *The Foreigner* (Delhi: Hind Pocket Books, 1972), p. 207.
2. T.S. Eliot, "East Coker," p. 147.
3. Arun Joshi, *The Strange Case of Billy Biswas* (Delhi: Hind Pocket Books, 1971), p. 8.
4. Arun Joshi, *The Apprentice* (New Delhi: Orient Paperbacks, 1974), p. 146.
5 Percy Lubbock, *The Craft of Fiction* (1921; rpt. London: Jonathan Cape, 1965), p. 140.
6. Gabriel Josipovici, *The World and the Book* (Frogmore: Paladin, 1973), p. 314.
7. Jorge Luis Borges, "The House of Asterion," trans. James E. Irby, in *Labyrinths*, p. 172.
8. Arun Joshi, *The Last Labyrinth* (New Delhi: Orient Paperbacks, 1981), p. 48.

Anita Desai and the Wounded Self

Anita Desai's modernist novels have received wide publicity and favourable critical response for their formal coherence and lyrical texture. But what is more interesting is the way in which the lyrical texture of her novels unravels the complexity associated with women who are burdened with the problems they confront in negotiating with a network of familial relations. The following passage from *Fire on the Mountain* illustrates the point:

> The old house, the full house, of that period of her life when she was the Vice-Chancellor's wife and at the hub of a small but intense and busy world, had not pleased her. Its crowding had stifled her. . . .
>
> There had been too many guests coming and going, tongas and rickshaws piled up under the eucalyptus trees and the bougainvilleas, their drivers asleep on the seats with their feet hanging over the bars. The many rooms of the house had always been full, extra beds would have had to be made up, often in not very private corners of the hall or veranda, so that there was a shortage of privacy that vexed her. Too many trays of tea would have to be made and carried to her husband's study, to her mother-in-law's bedroom, to the veranda that was the gathering-place for all, at all times of the day. Too many meals, too many dishes on the table, too much to wash up after.
>
> They had had so many children, they had gone to so many different schools and colleges at different times of the day, and had so many tutors—one for mathematics who was harsh and slapped the unruly boys, one for drawing who was lazy

> and smiled and did nothing, and others equally incompetent and irritating. Then there had been their friends, all of different ages and sizes and families.[1]

The passage unmistakably suggests the loss of privacy a housewife experiences in discharging what society thinks to be her responsibility. Nanda Kaul feels that her life as the wife of a Vice-Chancellor is "like a great, heavy, difficult book that she had read through and was not required to read again." (30) She is afraid that her great-granddaughter's visit to her may force her to open the "troublesome ledger" (30) again. The reasons for her fear and disinclination to get involved in a network of family relations are obvious. She has lived in an "intense and busy world." The repetition of the word "many" graphs the shortage of privacy that vexes her and the crowding that stifles her. That the family is an essential part of a woman's expanding consciousness—and however disinclined she may be to reopen the past, the past has inseparable link with the present—is clearly orchestrated in the following passage from *Clear Light of Day:*

> With her inner eye she saw how her own house and its particular history linked and contained her as well as her whole family with all their separate histories and experiences—not binding them within some dead and airless cell but giving them the soil in which to send down their roots, and food to make them grow and spread, reach out to new experiences and new lives, but always drawing from the same soil, the same secret darkness. That soil contained all time, past and future, in it. It was dark with time, rich with time. It was where her deepest self lived, and the deepest selves of her sister and brothers and all those who shared that time with her.[2]

In this passage, Bim, in a mood of intense reminiscence, accounts for the significance of "house" and "family" in maturing one's awareness and experience of the complexity and richness enshrined in familial relations. While Nanda Kaul thinks her past to be a "troublesome ledger" and doesn't want to reopen it, Bim in *Clear Light of Day* feels a metaphysical thrill in thinking that "it was where her deepest self lived, and the deepest selves of her sister and brothers and all those who shared that tie with her." Sita in *Where Shall We Go This Summer?*, in order to avoid giving birth to another child, leaves her home and stays in an island where she has a house she inherited from her father. When her husband goes there to take her to the city, she tells him that one of her profound experiences of joy was when she beheld a couple in the Hanging Gardens. The couple were so absorbed in each other that they were like a work of art, and she adds:

> They were not like us—they were inhuman, divine. They were so white, so radiant, they made me see my own life like a shadow, absolutely flat, uncoloured. That, that was the only—the only happy. . . .[3]

Raman, her husband, made uneasy by her strange words, tells her, "Any woman—any one would think you inhuman. You have four children. You have lived comfortably, always, in my house. You've not had worries. Yet your happiest memory is not of your children or your home but of strangers, seen for a moment, some lovers in a park. Not even of your own children." (147) Sita, in a distracted mood, says, "Children only mean anxiety, concern—pessimism. Not happiness. What other women call happiness is just sentimentality." (147) To Sita familial happiness or happiness in general doesn't consist in a harmonious existence with one's near and dear. It is just sentimentality. Maya, Anita Desai's protagonist in *Cry, the Peacock*, causes the death of her husband, Gautama, in her struggle to achieve what Sita calls sentimental.

The foregoing comments on Anita Desai's characters clearly demonstrate that most of her protagonists suffer from an extreme sort of self-introversion. We may not be wrong in saying that they are an intelligent but obsessed lot. The obsessions generate sometimes from a disharmonious family background, as we have it in *Voices in the City* and *Clear Light of Day;* in *Where Shall We Go This Summer?* and *Fire on the Mountain*, the obsessions are the consequence of the protagonists's craving for undisturbed introversion and introspection. Anita Desai's themes seem to direct her narrative mode, which we may call psycho-narration. But when she negotiates with a public theme, she employs the traditional narrative mode, which we notice in her novel, *In Custody*. Deven's struggle to capture and preserve the glory of Nur's Urdu poems leads to a shocking revelation, the deteriorating socio-cultural values.

Voices in the City dramatizes the waste-land motif of the city as a place that generates intense aridity of feeling and frustration. The atmosphere of the city, which dissolves all values of life and makes life amorphous, is suggested by the following passage:

> Striding off the bridge into the coagulated blaze of light and sound and odour that was the city of Calcutta, Nirode cried: Unfair, life is unfair—and how faint and senseless it sounded in all that tumult of traffic and commerce about him. In the darkness of that unfairness he saw Arun's future as an undimming brightness. . . . He remained in the half-dark—and each light on that street served to show up an expanse of wall, a doorway, a balcony that was darkly shadowed—and bled with longing to go; Arun had gone. Here he was still, the anonymous and shabby clerk on a newspaper, calling himself a journalist, for that is a fine, crisp and jaunty word. But the dismal truth was that all he did was cut out long strips of newspaper and paste and file them, occasionally venturing out to verify a dull fact in some airless office-room. Arun would be at a college in London, amongst students, in beer-halls—Nirode fought that vision of student-life abroad, that splendid vision that so dazzles those who do not know it.[4]

The above passage conveys in halting rhythms Nirode's disgust, and implicitly suggests that the cause and the effect are one. Nirode's mind is obsessed with the idea that life is unfair to him but at the same time it appears to be sensitive, perhaps too sensitive, to his brother's future as "undimming brightness." The lights in the street are contrasted with the darkness that ensues from life's unfairness. The obsessive notion of life's unfairness makes him brood over his own position as "the anonymous and shabby clerk on a newspaper, calling himself a journalist." Nirode's disgust with himself and his frustration are the consequences of the self recoiling from an intense feeling of righteousness wedded to an ideal. The following passage very well exemplifies the cynicism that vitiates all enterprise:

> The book he had meant to write, once he had created the proper conditions for the writing of it, seemed no more urgent now than it had one misty autumn night long ago when he had first thought of this plan. Nothing existed but this void in which all things appeared equally insignificant, equally worthless. Would he one day, he wondered, walk to the temple at the edge of this void, lay himself down on the flagstones smoothed and oiled by the passage of so many worshippers, bow his head at the feet of an inscrutably smiling idol and, inhaling the dense smog of incense, give himself up to the tolling of bells and a silent, shapeless god? The question had no substance, for Nirode knew he would never approach a god housed in a temple bustling with libidinous priests, vendors of garlands and plaster images, and women perspiring with piety. That odour of hair-oil, joss sticks and decaying flowers, the odour of worship, made his stomach heave. (63)

Nirode's void, "in which all things appeared equally insignificant, equally worthless," emerges from an awkward and embarrassing domestic tension. As a practising poet and journalist, Nirode moves among the budding poets of the city, who have poor wit and imagination: "He longed to remind them of the two rights Baudelaire had added to the rights of man—'the right to contradict oneself, and the right to leave'." (71) The "void," in the earlier passage, and "the two rights Baudelaire added to the rights of man," in the preceding passage, are fused in a subtle manner in Nirode's consciousness, which is distorted by family politics. Baudelaire's cynicism was the effect of his mother's second marriage. As a boy, he adored and loved his mother so intensely that her second marriage shattered his heart and damaged his psyche. His dandy exterior could not conceal his inner misery. Nirode's heart also has a similar chink, but it is more visible than Baudelaire's. He dislikes his mother for becoming the mistress of Major Chadha. Nirode's void and his cynicism stem from his mother's betrayal of the family prestige. His tough-guy attitude makes him vulnerable to the seedy atmosphere in which he lives.

Nirode's pretensions and pretexts as the budding Baudelaire of the city make him edit a magazine called *Voice*, which provides an opportunity for all seedy poets of the city to rush into print. He often mocks them and mocks himself and thereby betrays his lack of conviction in any healthy and sober enterprise. He seems to take unjustifiable pride in parading his over-burdened conscience. No wonder, he esteems Baudelaire, the arch-poet of modernism and the city. But Nirode is not a Baudelaire. His problems are too personal and his notions are too obsessive and erratic to find a steady and mature articulation. His study of Camus helps him little, for he does not assimilate the existential postulates to his scheme of values. Discussing Camus with his sister Amla, he says, "He wrote that 'in default of inexhaustible happiness, eternal suffering would at least give us a destiny. But we do not even have that consolation, and our worst agonies come to an end one day'." (184) He writes a play and gives it to his elder sister, Monisha. After reading it, she writes in her diary:

> Knowing Nirode as he was in these years after he ran away from college and floundered about in such torment, I would have thought him capable of precisely that action without regard for the fruit of action which the *Gita* tells us is the finest wisdom of all. So was his action when he worked on that grim newspaper, so was his action even when he edited his own magazine. But this play has trapped him at last. And he is more involved with mother and the past than I had suspected. Cast away involvement, I plead with him silently, cast it away and be totally empty, totally alone. (129)

Any reader would feel uneasy, though not surprised, when Monisha commits suicide. But it is surprising that Monisha's suicide brings about a sudden change in her brother's attitude towards everything, including his mother. Monisha's suicide may be taken as a physical enactment of Nirode's comment on Camus, which we have cited earlier. But his mental squint makes him unaware of his own contradictions, although he claims the right which Baudelaire added to the rights of man, viz., the right to contradict oneself. In the case of Baudelaire, the assertion of the right to contradict oneself takes the form of the symbolic enactment of the self searching for a principle of affirmation in the city, where the possibility of such an affirmation is fast dwindling.

The Baudelaire-Camus-*Gita* strand in the narrative, involving Nirode and his sisters, dramatizes the inward turn the self takes because of the tormenting and turbulent external world and suggests that this inward turn does not lead the self to the felicity and harmony that it longs for. The aberrations we notice in Nirode and in Monisha have their roots in the family disharmony, which is aggravated by the seedy society in which they find themselves. Monisha's diary very well illustrates the point. Married into a joint family, she finds herself crossed and contradicted on every occasion, and her privacy terribly violated. The following passage reinforces the point:

> I am glad they give me so much work to do. I am glad to be occupied in cutting vegetables, serving food, brushing small children's hair. Only I wish I were given some tasks I could do alone, in privacy, away from the aunts and uncles, the cousins and nieces and nephews. Alone, I could work better, and I should feel more—whole. But less and less there is privacy. (115-16)

The focus in the above passage is on the strong sense of preserving one's privacy as far as possible. But not only the home, the city also seems to encroach on the self and deprive it of the privacy it longs for. Monisha is seriously troubled and disturbed by the uneasy lassitude of conscience that is ubiquitous in the city, and she imagines it to be ghostly and toothless being that grins at her. It is this kind of obsessive and innate antipathy towards civil actuality that unnerves and drives Monisha to suicide. She cannot withstand a group of roadside singers performing their usual show. Just before she immolates herself, she feels:

> I am standing here, pressing myself against the wall so as not to feel senior aunt's flesh bump into me. I could not bear to have her touch me while she is sighing and humming and swaying to this loud music. I could not bear to touch, however vicariously, this appalling exhibition of a passion that ravages the soul and body and being. If I did, I should be a traitor, and a liar. I have never been touched by it, nor ravaged. I bear no scar on my body. I am different from them all. They put me away in a steel container, a thick glass cubicle, and I have lived in it all my life, without a touch of love or hate or warmth on me. (239)

The narrative irony in the novel is such that the self turned inward, which is like a self kept in a steel container or a thick glass cubicle, does not acquire detachment or non-involvement. But it is conscious, may be too conscious, of the causes that make it court alienation and aloofness. The inwardness of the self which Monisha searches for escapes her, largely because of her failure to educate it according to the ethics of the *Gita*. Nirode seems to acquire it by coming out of his self-imposed solitude and by seeing in his mother the goddess *Kali*, the Mother of all humanity. He tells his younger sister, Amla, "Oh, I see so clearly now, I feel my skin is stripped away and *my interior has melted into the exterior*, I know it so well. I see now that she is everything we have been fighting against, you and Monisha and I, and she is also everything we have fought for." (256, emphasis added)

Voices in the City explores the life of the middle- and the lower middle-classes of a city which is densely populated. Sociologically speaking, the seedy and nauseating industrial backdrop seems to play a crucial role in generating various kinds of mental aberrations and psychic disorders. Nirode's wounded self, Monisha's agonized self, and Amla's insecure self fail to cope with the continuous violence inherent in the "cityscape" meticulously evoked and stabilized in the novel. The vision that Nirode earns may provide the badly-needed healing touch to Nirode's wounded self. But in the case of the other women protagonists of Anita Desai it is not obviously there. *Fire on the Mountain* very well illustrates the point. Nanda Kaul, through whose consciousness the violent events of *Fire on the Mountain* are filtered, suffers from an intense awareness of lost privacy and the self's eagerness to recover and rehabilitate it. The following passage very well dramatizes her problem and her struggle:

> She would barely have splashed her face with some water and combed out her hair when the baby would come crawling in, the first to hear her stir, the most insistent in its needs. Lifting it into her arms, she would go to the kitchen to see the milk taken out of the ice-box, the layer of cream drawn off, the row of mugs on a tray filled and carried out to the green table on the veranda around which the children already sat on their low cane stools—the little girls still having their long hair plaited and their fresh cotton dresses buttoned, and the boys throwing themselves backwards and kicking the table legs and clamouring with hunger. Then there was the bread to be spread with butter, jam jars opened and dug into, knives taken away from babies and boys, girls questioned about home-work, servants summoned to mop up spilt milk and fetch tea, and life would swirl on again, in an eddy, a whirlpool of which she was the still, fixed eye in the centre. (24)

The above passage may be taken as a description of the normal duties and responsibilities of a housewife. But the images that conclude the paragraph, especially the image of the whirlpool, make the passage somewhat tense in tone. She is conscious of the monotonous "swirl" of life which she experienced as the wife of a Vice-Chancellor. After her husband's death she comes to Kasauli and stays at Carignano. She gets used to the still and solemn surroundings of the house and practises "stillness" and composure, which are supposed to act as a balm to her wounded self. The only visitor is Ila Das. Nanda Kaul's family and Ila Das's family were in close contact even before they come to renew it in Kasauli. She and Ila Das used to play together and go to school together, but Nanda Kaul cannot approve of her whole-heartedly. Her reservations about Ila Das stem from an attitude that is rather rigid. Moreover, Ila Das talks about things which Nanda Kaul dislikes. When Ila Das tells her, "Darling, I am growing o-o-old!" (117) Nanda Kaul feels terribly upset:

> The entire weight of the overloaded past seemed to pour onto her like liquid cement that immediately set solid, incarcerating her in its stiff gloom. She sat with her lips tightly set. (117)

But Ila Das discharges her duties as a Welfare Officer in the area promptly and efficiently. It is her passion for justice, change, and reform that brings her trouble. She is assaulted, raped, and killed because she prevents a child marriage. When P.K. Shukla, the police officer in charge of the area, informs Nanda Kaul about the murder of Ila Das, the news shocks and kills her. It is at this moment that she becomes acutely aware of the discrepancy between what society thinks of her want and what in fact she is. Her silent and unspoken confession betrays her wounded self:

> Nor had her husband loved and cherished her and kept her like a queen—he had only done enough to keep her quiet while he carried on a lifelong affair with Miss David, the mathematics mistress, whom he had not married because she was a Christian but whom he had loved, all his life loved. And her children—the children were all alien to her nature. She neither understood nor loved them. She did not live here alone by choice—she lived here alone because that was what she was forced to do, *reduced to doing*. (145, emphasis added)

Now it is clear that Nanda Kaul, surviving with a wounded self, tries to cultivate a measure of composure in her struggle to forget the wound caused by her husband's indiscretion. She is afraid of the past, and her great granddaughter Raka's visit once again plunges her into the past and reopens the wound. Raka also seems to suffer from an oppressive memory associated with her parents. There seems to be no love lost between Raka's mother, Tara, and her husband, who is an officer in the Indian Foreign Service. Her father, having failed to "socialize" her mother, ceases to take interest in her even as a patient. When Raka beholds through a chink in the door what is going on inside the club on the mountain, she feels that

> Somewhere behind them, behind it all, was her father, home from a party, stumbling and crashing through the curtains of night, his mouth opening to let out a flood of rotten stench, beating at her mother with hammers and fists of abuse." (71)

It is in one of her secret trips to the mountain that she sees a huge fire devastating the dried vegetation below, in the valley. The death of Nanda Kaul, caused by the unhappy fate of Ila Das, seems to be a thematic variation and a symbolic concomitant of the fire Raka causes on the mountain. The fire that her father's behaviour creates inside Raka suggests that the wounded self which Anita Desai portrays in her fiction is a consequence of a disharmonious and sometimes violently disturbed family atmosphere. Most of her protagonists, in a state of nervous breakdown, turn inward for a healing touch which sometimes they find, as we have seen in the case of Nirode in *Voices in the City*. We notice an identical pattern in *Clear Light of Day*.

Clear Light of Day dramatizes the story of a family of two brothers and two sisters. Raja is a poet, who marries a Muslim girl and lives in Hyderabad, keeping a tenuous connection with his brother and sisters, who live in Delhi. Baba is a mentally retarded person, who always stays at home and enjoys obsolete music from gramophone records. Bimla works as a lecturer in a Delhi college and nurses an eternal grievance against her brother for deserting the family. Tara, her sister, marries an officer in the civil service, leaving Baba and Bimla to seek their own salvation in the ancestral house. It is Tara's visit to the ancestral house with her husband and children that makes Bimla revive the past and reflect on it.

Bimla, the central consciousness in *Clear Light of Day*, whose self is wounded by the callous behaviour of her parents and her brother, very often compares her relations and their memory to mosquitoes. The following excerpts from her reminiscence clarify her feeling:

> The memory came whining out of the dark like a mosquito, dangling its long legs and hovering just out of reach. (151)
>
> The mosquitoes that night were like the thoughts of the day embodied in monster form, invisible in the dark but present everywhere, most of all in and around the ears, piercingly audible. (152)
>
> They had come like mosquitoes—Tara and Bakul, and behind them the Misras, and somewhere in the distance Raja and Benazir—only to torment her and, mosquito-like, sip her blood. All of them fed on her blood, at some time or the other had fed—it must have been good blood, sweet and nourishing. Now, when they were full, they rose in swarms, humming away, turning their backs on her. (153)

The above citations suggest the pattern of Bimla's feelings. Ironically enough, she doesn't articulate her feelings. But Dr. Biswas, who comes to treat Raja, diagnoses Bimla's predicament and says, "Now I understand why you do not wish to marry. You have dedicated your life to others—to your sick brother and your aged aunt and your little brother who will be dependent on you all his life. You have sacrificed your own life for them." (97) Although the narrator seems to think that Dr. Biswas misunderstands Bimla, we are not wrong in inferring that somewhere in her consciousness Bimla's frustration crystallizes itself into tiny spot, which gradually develops into a perpetual and unhealed wound. The domestic disharmony that often stifles and chokes Bimla's adventurous spirit has as its objective correlative the fortunes of the two girls, Jaya and Sarla, in the Misra family. The Misras are Bimla's neighbours. Though the girls are married at an early age, they are abandoned by their husbands. Talking about the familial life of the Misra boys,

Bimla says:

> The wives wanted the new life, they wanted to be modern women. I think they wanted to move into their own separate homes, in New Delhi, and cut their hair short and give card parties, or open boutiques or learn modelling. They can't stand our sort of Old Delhi life—the way the Misras vegetate here in the bosom of the family. So they spend as much time as they can away. (151)

Though Bimla's comment refers to the Misra boys, it applies with equal force to her parents, her brother, and sister. Moreover, Bimla's resolve not to marry is firmly rooted in her domestic circumstances. The following conversation between Bimla and Tara about the Misra girls illustrates the point:

> "Their mother wanted them to be married soon. She said she married when she was twelve and Jaya and Sarla are already sixteen and seventeen years old."
>
> "But they're not *educated* yet," Bim said sharply. "They haven't any degrees. They should go to college," she insisted.
>
> "Why?" said Tara. . . .
>
> "Why?" repeated Bim indignantly. 'Why, because they might find marriage isn't enough to last them the whole of their lives," she said darkly, mysteriously.
>
> "What else could there be?" countered Tara. "I mean," she fumbled, "for them."
>
> "What *else*?" asked Bim. "Can't you think? I can think of hundreds of things to do instead. *I* won't marry," she added, very firmly.
>
> Tara glanced at her sideways with a slightly sceptical smile.
>
> "I won't," repeated Bim, adding "I shall never leave Baba and Raja and Mira-*masi*." (140)

The above dialogue does not reveal Bimla's confidence in herself but only exposes her wounded self. Almost a similar feeling, perhaps more mature recognition and acknowledgement of the implications of her resolve, is suggested by the following passage:

> All these years she had felt herself to be the centre—she had watched them all circling in the air, then returning, landing like birds, folding up their wings and letting down their legs till they touched solid ground. Solid ground. That was what the house had been—the lawn, the rose walk, the guava trees, the veranda: Bim's domain. The sound of Baba's gramophone and the pigeons. Summer days and nights. In winter, flower-beds and nuts and cotton quilts. Aunt Mira and the dog, roses and the cat—and Bim. Bim, who had stayed, and become part of the pattern, inseparable. They had needed her as much as they had needed the sound of the pigeons in the veranda and the ritual of the family gathering on the lawn in the evening. (153)

The above passage, the most revealing in the text, graphs the development of Bimla's expanding consciousness. Unlike Maya in *Cry, the Peacock*, Monisha in *Voices in the City*, Nanda Kaul in *Fire on the Mountain*, and Sita in *Where Shall We Go This Summer?*, Bimla's wounded self discovers the soothing balm and the healing touch at home and in the family. She becomes a part of a pattern, and the pattern consists in her realizing the importance of her relationship with the lawn, the rose walk, the guava trees, the flower-beds, the dog, the pigeons, aunt Mira, Baba, and the sound of Baba's gramophone. It is this inclusive vision of the self's affiliations with the family and society that enriches the experience, harmonizes the self's connections with the family and society, and makes the self bathe in "clear light of day."

The two epigraphs, from Emily Dickinson and T.S. Eliot, prefixed to the narrative, signify the role of memory in achieving adequate awareness of the theme of the loss and renewal of the self. While Eliot's lines from *Little Gidding* emphasize the pattern that emerges as a result of the process of the loss and renewal, Emily Dickinson's lines suggest that memory is capable of celebrating the gain and consoling the loss at one and the same time. The repeated allusion to Eliot's *Four Quartets* in the text is more suggestive of a pattern that may emerge in the self negotiating with its own problems than any kind of affirmation about the self's supremacy or maturity.

In Custody again is a re-creation of the problems and the agonies of the wounded self. Unlike the novels that we have discussed so far, *In Custody* has at its centre an ineffectual but well-meaning young man whose problems are not just personal and private but public and social. Deven Sharma, a temporary Hindi lecturer in Lala Ram Lal College at Mirpor, has great passion for Urdu poetry. The narrative is organized in such a way that the cultural past of India becomes part and parcel of the bubbling and throbbing consciousness of Deven. The town Mirpore has a Muslim area and a Hindi area, dominated by the mosque and the temple respectively. Deven's friend Murad, who edits an Urdu journal, *Awaaz*, from New Delhi, prevails on him to write an article on Nur's poetry for his journal. Though his financial circumstances do not permit him to make a trip to Delhi, the temptation to acquire name and fame by writing something on a celebrated Urdu poet like Nur propels Deven to commit himself to the task. When Murad's boy takes him to Chandni Chowk in order to have an interview with Nur, Deven finds himself in an alien and suffocating atmosphere. Though the poet is impressed by Deven's clean and chaste pronunciation, he is not in a position to discuss his poetry with Deven because his mind is not on poetry but on the ways and means of tackling people who swarm round him for various reasons. Deven is impressed not by Nur's latest poetry, which is absolutely nil, but by his still active and virile imagination. To Deven, Nur is a significant poet not because he makes things immediate but because he removes them to a position where they become bearable:

> That was what Nur's verse did—placed frightening and inexplicable experiences like time and death at a point where they could be seen and studied, in safety.[5]

While Deven's aesthetic sensibility moves in the right direction, his confidence in translating it into a written document slowly dwindles, for Nur's health, the riff-raff that gathers round him every evening, and the incessant friction between his wives are the insurmountable obstacles any admirer of Nur has to face. The social and the cultural significance of *In Custody* in terms of the self consists in Deven's honest efforts to surmount these insurmountable obstacles.

Encouraged by his friend Murad and a liberal grant from the college authorities, Deven arranges to record Nur's views on poetry and a few poems which he may recite from memory. But the whole thing misfires because the tape-recorder doesn't work properly and the assistant sent by Murad doesn't know how to operate the recorder. Deven spends the money given by the college authorities not only to procure the recorder but also to feed Nur and gratify the lady who arranges the whole show. The ostensible aim of the entire enterprise is to keep the tapes on which Nur's voice is recorded in the college library for the pleasure and benefit of all lovers of Urdu poetry. But when the tapes are played, they produce neither a coherent dialogue nor the recitation of poems but a nonsensical jumble of voices. Cheated by his friends and suffering from the pangs of failure, Deven feels:

> He could lead the rest of his life in this near-unconscious state. He hoped his former life of non-events, non-happenings, would be resumed, empty and hopeless, safe and endurable. That was the only life he was made for, although life was not perhaps the right term. He needed one that was more grey, more neutral, more shadowy. He sifted through alternatives like torn pieces of grey paper, letting them fall to the floor of his mind with a whisper and bury him in sleep. (183-84)

The events that precede the hopeless position in which Deven is trapped emerge from a cultural matrix and a social milieu over which Deven has no control. The following passage very well illustrates the truth of the foregoing observation.

> Turning his mind decisively away from these dangerous shoals, he paced up and down in his bare feet, his pyjamas and

> the vest full of holes, scratching at mosquito bites, smoking an occasional cigarette, refusing to entertain poetry and thinking in strict prose that he must look like a caged animal in a zoo to any creature that might be looking down at earth from another planet. And that was all he was—a trapped animal. In his youth, he had had the illusion of having free will, not knowing he was in a trap. Marriage, a family and a job had placed him in this cage; now there was no way out of it. The unexpected friendship with Nur had given him the illusion that the door of the trap had opened and he could escape after all into a wider world that lay outside but a closer familiarity with the poet had shown him that what he thought of as "the wider world" was an illusion too—it was only a kind of zoo in which he could not hope to find freedom, he would only blunder into another cage inhabited by some other trapped animal. Being an illustrious poet had drawn people to the zoo to come and stare at him but Nur had not escaped from his cage for all that—he was as trapped as Deven was even if his cage was more prominent and attracted more attention. Still, it was just a cage in a row of cages. Cage, cage. Trap, trap. (131)

The above passage, with its recurring emphasis on "trap" and "cage," brings to a central focus the private and the public themes. Deven's efforts to escape from the cage of marriage, a family, and a job land him in the public world of Urdu poetry and intellectual fame. But that wider world itself is a kind of zoo in which he finds the poet attracting public attention. Whether it is the private world or the public world, the self doesn't find freedom for itself, for the obvious reason that the forces that control the two worlds are beyond its control. Even after the failure of the entire project, Deven is under social pressure. His students, who help him to restore a semblance of coherence in the tapes, demand first division marks. Nur writes to him for medical allowance and an endowment for his child from the college authorities. Murad wants him to complete his article on Nur. Reeling under various kinds of pressures and demands, Deven feels that "He had imagined he was taking Nur's poetry into safe custody, and not realized that if he was to be custodian of Nur's genius, then Nur would become his custodian and place him in custody too. This alliance could be considered an unendurable burden—or else a shining honour. Both demanded an equal strength." (203)

The epigraph prefixed to the novel, taken from Wordsworth's "Rob Roy's Grave," suggests the ironic perspective that controls the narrative. In Wordsworth's poem, the speaker feels that the Scotch thief, who was brave and wise, entered society "an age too late:/Or shall we say an age too soon?"[6] for the obvious reason that his love of freedom, or liberty, has to encounter a society dominated by "rents and factors, rights of chance,/Sheriffs, and lairds and their domains."[7] Rob Roy felt that books and statutes are the barriers that man himself placed against the self. Like Rob Roy, the free spirit of Deven longs for freshness and stimulation at the time when social civility has deteriorated into social uncivility. It is not social uncivility that wounds Deven, but his intrinsic compulsions. The compulsions emerge from his domestic and financial circumstances, which make it impossible for him to keep what he has achieved. The locale and the atmosphere which are foregrounded in the text consist of a city with endless slums, hawkers, beggars, shopkeepers, and swindlers, all busy in their own way, transforming poetry into shocking and turbulent prose. Cold-shouldered by one of his colleagues when he approaches him for help, Deven feels:

> He could not see why anyone should help him. He no longer knew if he ought to be—or even if he wanted to be helped. Were these people really helping him to succeed in a unique and wonderful enterprise or simply locking him up more and more firmly in a barred trap? And was the trap set by Murad, by Siddiqui, or by Nur and his wives. All he knew was that he who had set out to hunt Nur down was being hunted down himself, the prey. (143)

If we gloss the passage in terms of the epigrapn prefixed to the novel, it becomes ironical, in the sense that among Deven and his friends neither Rob Roy's primitive social dynamic nor that of the

French revolutionists, who are alluded to in the poem, prevails. But what is significant and revealing is Deven's determined effort to keep what he has achieved and, in the process, heal the wounded self. While Wordsworth's Rob Roy thought of vindicating the self by visualizing a state of society much later described and advocated by Rousseau, Deven tries to salvage the self by patiently resisting the social and the anti-social forces. In spite of the crises he faces, "He thought of Nur's poetry being read, the sound of it softly murmuring in his ears. He had accepted *the gift* of Nur's poetry and that meant he was custodian of Nur's very soul and spirit. It was a great distinction. He could not deny or abandon that under *any pressure.*" (204, emphasis added) Nur's gift to Deven is not an object, a system, or a creed but a sensibility that can ruminate repeatedly on a couplet like "The breeze enters, the blossom on the bough wafts its scent./The opened window lets in the sweet season, spring. (106)

The texts of Anita Desai we have discussed and analyzed are remarkable not only for their stylistic alchemy but also for their socio-cultural commentary on modern modes of existence. City life in India, in all its variety and detail, constitutes a large chunk of her writing. Calcutta, New Delhi and Old Delhi, and Bombay are not actualities but are the re-created images of the Indian social scene in *Voices in the City*, *Clear Light of Day*, *In Custody*, and *Where Shall We Go This Summer?* Breathing the polluted air of the city, her characters try to escape from their cages sometimes successfully and sometimes not, and in the process get themselves mentally bruised and spiritually battered. The narrative base in Anita Desai's texts is the family. As Robert D. Hess and Gerald Handel have observed, "The family's life together is an endless process of movement in and around consentual understanding, from attachment to conflict and withdrawal—and over again. Separateness and connectedness are the underlying conditions of a family's life, and its common task is to give form to both."[8] Anita Desai's narratives not only give shape to separateness and connectedness that emerge from a family saga, but dramatize the way in which the self receives wound, which are either aggravated or healed by the socio-cultural matrix, which is its soil and sustenance.

NOTES

1. Anita Desai, *Fire on the Mountain* (New Delhi: Allied, 1977), pp. 29-30.
2. Anita Desai, *Clear Light of Day* (New Delhi: Allied, 1980), p. 182.
3. *Where Shall We Go This Summer?* (Delhi: Orient Paperbacks, 1982), pp. 146-47.
4. Anita Desai, *Voices in the City* (Delhi: Orient Paperbacks, 1985), pp. 8-9.
5. Anita Desai, *In Custody* (London: Heinemann, 1984), p. 54.
6. William Wordsworth, "Rob Roy's Grave," *The Poetical Works of Wordsworth*, ed. Thomas Hutchinson, rev. ed. De Selincourt (1936; rpt. London: Oxford University Press, 1959), pp. 231-232, 64-65.
7. *Ibid.*, pp. 69-70.
8. Robert D. Hess and Gerald Handel, "The Family as a Psychological Organization," in *The Psychological Interior of the Family*, ed. Gerald Handel (Chicago, 1967), p. 10.

Conclusion

I

Roger Sharrock, in *The Figure in a Landscape*, says that a poet is "not a camera, but a consciousness."[1] This profound observation is very useful in analyzing not only poems but all creative writing. The novels that we have analyzed in the preceding chapters are not photographs of life as it is lived; they are re-creation of life as perceived and transformed by the novelists's perception and imagination. A novelist as a person need not conform himself to a system of values, but as a creative writer his consciousness is moulded by a sort of value system. The novelists we have discussed are serious artists but are not committed to any one system, except that of the self and its relation with other selves. A sociologist may think that society derives its form not from individual "selves" but from the functions these "selves" perform. But a creative writer's idea of the self emerges from his consciousness and acquires a shape and a vision by being made an organic part of a dramatic action which is meaningful. Most modernist writers, while dramatizing life as a struggle between opposites like the sacred and the secular, faith and lack of faith, society and individual, artist and man, integration and alienation, the outer and the inner, seem to forge an aesthetic in which these opposites are reconciled, or at least remain in a state of mutual coexistence. Of the novelists under review, Anita Desai and Arun Joshi appear to be modernist, while Rajan, Raja Rao, and Narayan appear to be traditional, in the sense that the aesthetic we notice in their fictions is very much rooted in the Hindu tradition. But in all these writers we notice a felicitous fusion of the transcendental and the humanistic traditions in Indian thought.

Apart from these novelists, writers like Kamala Markandaya, Bhabani Bhattacharya, to mention only two significant names, dramatize actions in which the self, the family and society are sometimes in conflict and sometimes in harmony. In a sequence of novels culminating in *Pleasure City*, Kamala Markandaya's stories deal with social justice and injustice, poverty and principle, faith and lack of it, the East and the West, and individual and society. A good example that could be cited is *A Handful of Rice.* Ravi's migration from a village to a town, his growing acquaintance with another young man, Damodar, who is a part of the black market racket, his association with Appu's family, his marriage with Nalini, Appu's daughter, his decline as a member of society, and his struggle between the tempting luxury Damodar gives for joining hands with him and the unbearable poverty he faces are typical of any fiction that tries to convey the tragic sense of Indian life. Bhabani Bhattacharya's *So Many Hungers!* conveys with remarkable subtlety the view that the great Bengal famine was partly the result of vicious economic exploitation. The feeling of the central character, Kajoli, is conveyed in the following passage, which is unmistakably representative:

> A fighter? Had she not yielded to her fate without a struggle? Become one with the maps of mindless destitutes? Feeding at the free kitchen. Picking from muck-heaps. No grit. A mere beggar-woman. And soon to die—die a thousand deaths.[2]

Unable to sustain themselves in a village ravaged by an unprecedented famine, Kajoli, her mother, and her brother go to Calcutta. In Calcutta, we notice various sorts of hunger prevailing. The poor are hungry for food, the exploiters are hungry for money, and the vicious characters are hungry for lewd pleasures. Kajoli sacrifices herself and her character just for satisfying the hunger of her poor, starving mother. A crude realist may say that it is a daily event in any third-world country. But the novelist creates the image of a society under pressure, in which other strains like unscrupulous exploitation and scant respect for the time-honoured values could be clearly seen.

II

Of the five novelists we have discussed, Rajan's novels present a society that is sophisticated and glamorous. But his characters involve themselves in contemporary issues like communal disharmony. As has been shown earlier, the contemporary issues and events are not in themselves significant. What is significant is the way in which they divide and unite characters who are groping in a hostile milieu for that sort of stability and social security in which they can enjoy their personal gains. The novels are organized on a very sensitive issue that still remains alive in the Indian social context, the arranged marriage. The problems that arise in an arranged marriage make Krishnan a divided self. The disruption and resumption of the Krishnan-Kamala relationship is an inclusive and significant thematic base that operates in terms of dualities which are part and parcel of the Hindu transcendental tradition enshrined in the *Gita*. Krishnan and his counterpart in *Too Long in the West*, Nalini, while coming into terms with the dualities, also acquire a state of selfhood, which makes the word "Brahmin" acquire transcendental connotations. It is here that the transcendental and the humanistic strains in the Hindu socio-cultural thought earn a symbolic meaning. Nataraja and His Consort create, sustain, and destroy the palpable world, of which the self is an organic unit. The Cosmic Dance is a perennial process in which Krishnans and Kamalas have their significance and reality. However much the sophistication imbibed from the West stands in the way of achieving an intrinsic integration of the self, the family, and society, the overall import of the Krishnan-Kamala relationship is that integration is possible.

Raja Rao's novels are more complex and ambitious than Rajan's. Raja Rao's characters are members of traditional Hindu Brahmin families. As Ramaswamy often says, "Brahmin is he who knows Brahman." Brahman is the Cosmic Self, in which each individual self beholds its own identity. But this is not a mere matter of words. It is more easily said than achieved. Raja Rao's fiction as a whole dramatizes the various socio-cultural changes which subject the traditional Hindu family and its values to a severe and honest probe. The caste-ridden Hindu society gives ample scope to Raja Rao to explore the tensions within society which are generated by the rigidity and the inflexibility of the caste system. Moreover, a traditional Brahmin's journey to the West, his stay in the West, and his return to the mother country give him an opportunity to assess objectively the meaning and the significance of his own values. There is a possibility, in the process of the reassessment of the alien values, of becoming conscious of what is vulnerable in one's self. A similar creative quest is seen among the European artists. As Robert S. Ellwood observes, "Many in our day have made the Journey to the East of Hermann Hesse's paradigmatic novel. For some, ostensibly, it has been a quest for that sort of knowledge which makes for power in the commercial or political worlds. For some, like certain of the Company in Hesse's novel, the search—often never physically leaving Europe—is the romantic quest for the Distant which unlocks the Past, the Sunrise East of ultimate origins—for the secret of one's lost identity, for the barely-remembered splendour of one's childhood world. Others, like the subject of the present paper, Percival Lowell (and more recently Arthur Koestler), have professed that the East has only sent them back to the West with renewed confidence in its values."[3] The foregoing observation suggests the possibility that an Indian after a prolonged stay in the West may return home with a renewed confidence in the values of Indian tradition and culture. What happens in Raja Rao's fiction is that his characters not only acquire a renewed confidence in their values but try to reorganize those values from a humanistic perspective. In the case of Moorthy and Govindan Nair, the humanistic perspective has an Indian origin, and in the case of Ramaswamy and Kirillov alias Padmanabha Iyer, it has a Western origin. The Independence struggle and the Gandhian social revolution inspire Moorthy in *Kanthapura* to do away with the caste system in spite of the protests of the traditional society. The conflict between the self and society in *Kanthapura* consists in the hostility that Moorthy's visits to the Harijan quarter provoke among the inmates of the Brahmin quarter. But it is Gandhi's humanism that helps Moorthy triumph in silencing his opponents who are indeed formidable. Govindan Nair in *The Cat and Shakespeare* seems to succeed in blending the transcendental and the humanistic in Indian thought by being faithful to both. Though a Nair, he has a profound knowledge of Indian transcendental thought, while Ramakrishna Pai, a Brahmin, does not have any of it. Govindan Nair exemplifies in himself the definition of a Brahmin as one who knows Brahman. His absolute confidence in Divine Mother symbolized by the mother cat helps him negotiate with all kinds of stormy weather. Keeping pain in one eye and joy in the other, he appears to be a man who has an intuitive knowledge of the self, and harmonizes its relationship with the family and society. Although he is aware of the shortcomings of his colleagues, acquaintances, and neighbours, his humanistic perspective influences him in showing a charitable disposition towards their lapses. To put it in a different way, Govindan Nair shows, in a remarkable way, the impersonal attitude of Shakespeare towards humanity, which is detached and at the same time compassionate.

In *The Serpent and the Rope,* Ramaswamy finds himself in a cosmopolitan setting and elitist society. He hops from place to place. Paris and London are the centres of his intellectual activity. As has been pointed our earlier, Ramaswamy is a typical example of an Indian whose journey to the West confirms the authenticity of Hindu society and its values. One may construe the misunderstanding and separation of Ramaswamy and Madeleine as an unnegotiable gulf between the East and the West. But this is not so. A mature understanding of the issue appears to be that Ramaswamy's self evolves from romantic notions to transcendental notions. To put it in a different way, the romantic self slowly but steadily evolves into the imperial self. Considering this transformation as a quest, we notice that the experience of familial and social relations stands him in good stead to proceed from academic, cultural, and romantic pursuits to the pursuit of the exploration of the self. In the novel, there is a sustained comparison and contrast between Georges and Catherine, and Ramaswamy and Madeleine as married couples. Apart from the advantages of sharing a common culture, Georges and Catherine have the additional advantage of pursuing activities which are in harmony with the society in which they live. We notice in the case of Madeleine and Ramaswamy a simmering dissatisfaction with each other's cultural background and in the case of Ramaswamy it is aggravated by his relationship with Savithri. Ramaswamy is very much aware when he thrusts marriage on his sister Saroja that the permissiveness that obtains in these matters in Western society is totally absent in Hindu society. But this does not in any way affect his faith in the sanctity and the inviolability of the self as embodied in the Hindu transcendental tradition. It is not surprising when he takes the decision to go and seek the feet of his *Guru* in Trivandrum. It is a time-honoured and established tradition in Hindu society that one should seek enlightenment from a *Guru*. The relationship between the master and the disciple is still the solid base on which the self can nourish and earn an inclusive vision of the self, the family, and society.

III

Narayan's Malgudi stories may be construed as a critique of the manners and morals of the South-Indian middle-class life. In all these stories, the family appears to be the centre of activity. Narayan's mild and gentle irony probes and reveals some of the common foibles of a middle-class Indian. As John Colmer rightly observes, "The successful critic of society, it may be suggested, is the writer who learns the wisdom of indirection. He is the writer who learns to combine instruction with delight, without in any way compromising his integrity of blunting the force of his social criticism."[4] The foregoing observation appears to be an apt description of Narayan the story teller. His characters like Margayya, Nataraj and his friend, Vasu, Raju and Rosie, Jagan, and Raman and Daisy are the products of a society the values of which are simple and direct. They may be reckoned as characters who struggle to preserve what they have and what they acquire. But, as it happens in life, it so happens in Narayan's comedy that the loss and the gain are the result of one's character and action, or, to put it in the Hindu way, the result of one's *karma*. It is in passing through the alternating phases of loss and gain that the self acquires stability and harmony. Narayan seems to advocate the view that evil, either social or metaphysical, has in itself the roots of its destruction. It may take a long time for the process to reach its completion. But in spite of the terrible hardships they face, most Hindus believe in the ultimate triumph of the *sattvik* elements in society. The foregoing idea is creatively presented in *The Man-Eater of Malgudi.* Although Vasu, a taxidermist and a local menace in the novel, may be construed as an embodiment of what is evil in man, there is a possibility of considering him as Narayan's creative comment on the subversion of values that operates in most commercial activities. The suggestive irony in a passage like the following cannot go unnoticed:

> I think there is a good business proposition here. I can supply them stuffed eagles at about fifty rupees each. Everyone can keep a sacred *Garuda* in the *puja* and I'll guarantee that it won't fly off. Thus they can save their eyes from glare. I want to be of service to our religious folk in my own way. (64)

The Financial Expert, apart from being an interesting story in itself, is a subtle comment on the fate of persons who like to climb the ladder from poverty to riches and leap from fortune to fortune. It also brings to the fore the various ways in which social welfare schemes are exploited to enrich private individuals. Jagan in *The Vendor of Sweets* is a typical Narayan character, in the sense that his Gandhian ethic doesn't prevent him in hoarding currency in the attic of his house and carrying his cheque-book wherever he goes. Raju in *The Guide*, in trying to exploit the resentment of a housewife against her husband, lands himself in an awkward situation from which he cannot disentangle himself. Raman, the painter of signs, propagates the virtue and the efficacy of family planning with the fond hope of acquiring a wife to beget children. This does not mean that Narayan is against the idea of family planning. It only suggests that there is an unnecessary fuss about a simple matter which could be tackled at the base level without terrorizing the village folk. When we construe a creative work as social criticism, we should not make the mistake of ignoring the value of a creative work as a creative work. Moreover, Narayan's irony, while providing the socio-critical insight, suggests that in fine, the self reposes itself in the stability of truth. A story like *A Tiger for Malgudi* reinforces the idea that any transcendental quest should necessarily be in harmony with an enlightened humanistic perspective. One of the ironies of the story appears to be that the animal world is more responsive to spiritual orientation than the human world. Man is eager to exploit the animal world for his own ends whereas an animal is not capable of it. The built-in ironies, such as those we have just noticed, make it hardly easy to subsume Narayan's stories under any fictional genre. Hence we think it not inappropriate to call the entire corpus of Narayan's fiction the comedy of the self.

IV

Robert Penn Warren, discussing the relevance of Faulkner, makes the following observation:

> This is where the question of the "relevance" of literature comes in. As a kind of short-hand, we may say that literature *may* carry a sort of built-in rebuke to the hubris of its age, and that the more powerful the drives of an age and the more successful they appear, the more powerful, radical, and complex may be the literature on "rebuke." For instance, we may cite the tragedy of Athens in the age that drove toward the debacle of Syracuse, or that of the Elizabethan period with its newly opened society of "ambition," the poetry of the English Romantics in the context of the Industrial Revolution, the work of Hawthorne and Melville in the society of the 1840s and '50s or that of Melville again, Mark Twain, and James in the Guilded Age, and of Dreiser in the age of Coolidge. Furthermore, such a "rebuke," though it may be literal and direct (as it often was, but not always, with Zola), is more apt to be "mythic" and "radical"—that is, to take a form which, because of its distance from the literal, may give a drama at once more strongly focussed than life ordinarily affords, and more deeply suggestive. As Aldous Huxley says of tragedy,

> such a "rebuke," whether tragic or not, gives only a half-truth; it gives only one, abstracted perspective on actuality, but that may be an essential truth, a "radical" truth, not to be ignored.[5]

Arun Joshi's fiction and its relevance may be construed by making use of some of the insights embodied in the above citation. His fiction carries a sort of built-in rebuke to the hubris of our age. *The Apprentice*, for example, is an incisive comment on the contemporary Indian scene, closely modelled on Albert Camus's *The Fall*. It unravels hypocrisy and corruption that are ubiquitous, although the protagonist's penitential role seems to salvage the crumbling self. Jean-Baptiste Clemence, the protagonist of *The Fall*, like Ratan Rahor of Joshi, sees the falsity of his existence and tries to salvage his fragmented self, christening himself judge-penitent. He narrates his experiences in such a way that the norms of our civility are placed in their proper perspective. In a revealing passage, he says, "He who clings to a law does not fear the judgement that puts him in his place within an order he believes in. But the keenest of human torments is to be judged without law. Yet we are in that torment. Deprived of their natural curb, the judges, loosed at random, are racing through their job. Hence we have to try to go faster than they, don't we? And it's a real mad house. Prophets and facts multiply; they hasten to get there with a good law or a flawless organization before the world is deserted. Fortunately, I arrived. I am the end and the beginning; I announce the law. In short, I am a judge-penitent."[6] Ratan Rathor narrates his experiences like Jean-Baptiste and although he doesn't call himself a penitent, the entire narrative, punctuated with words like "sham," "bogus," "fake," "whore," "humiliation," and their analogues, is an unreserved confession of the self which transforms penitence into prayer. The sort of penitential prayer we have just noticed is a characteristic of Joshi's maiden novel, *The Foreigner*. Sindi Oberoi passes through a therapeutic process in which he feels that an "indefatigable surgeon" (207) is cleaning up his soul with the sharp edge of his scalpel. This suggests that Joshi's protagonist, while submitting his self to a clinical probe, earns an awareness which makes his own self a labyrinth. The image of the labyrinth, as we have noticed earlier, controls the narrative perspective of Joshi's fiction. The consonance and the dissonance that characterize the self, the family, and society are metaphorically suggested and authenticated by the following passage from *The Strange Case of Billy Biswas:*

> If life's meaning lies not in the glossy surfaces of our pretensions but in those dark mossy labyrinths of the soul that languish forever, hidden from the dazzling light of the sun, then I do not know of any man who sought it more doggedly and, having received a signal, abandoned himself so recklessly to its call. In brief, I know of no other man who so desperately pursued the tenuous thread of existence to its bitter end, no matter what trails of glory or shattered hearts he left behind in his turbulent wake. (8)

In fine, Arun Joshi's fiction, without appearing as an overt sociological exercise, gathers within its fold most of the issues that trouble and torment the post-Independence generation. The way out of the labyrinth is not to make the self a mirror but to liberate it by constantly reminding oneself that the labyrinth is not an unsafe place to exist, provided one is apprenticed to the sublime principle of giving, which is very well exemplified in Anuradha in *The Last Labyrinth.*

Anita Desai's wounded self, which is dramatized largely in terms of a woman's world, doesn't expand in space and time but always turns inward. Familial disharmony brings in a kind of self-alienation, which in turn impels Desai's protagonists to subject themselves to a search for an emotional centre within, which they can cling to in their crises. *Voices in the City* dramatizes the inner dissonance in Nirode's family which is a consequence of his mother's indiscretion. The wounded self in Nirode in its outward emergence transforms itself and manifests as a cynical irreverence for all the traditional norms of social behaviour. His blistering frankness disturbs his friends and makes him feel that he lives in a hostile social milieu. An identical state of feeling we notice in Nanda Kaul. Even those Indians who stay abroad suffer from a sense of isolation and self privation. Kamala Markandaya's *The Nowhere Man* and Anita Desai's *Bye-Bye, Blackbird* converge on the theme of Indians abroad. In *The Nowhere Man*, Kamala Markandaya deliberately makes everything go against Srinivas, who has lived in London for over fifty years. Srinivas tries to evict his anti-Indian tenants on the plea that he is a leper and hence would like to isolate himself from everybody. But he doesn't succeed. He dies in a fire accident caused by Fred, who hates Indians. The tragic sense of life that emerges from *The Nowhere Man* makes one think that we haven't emancipated ourselves from the prejudices and the restraints of colonialism. An Indian in London is not a man but a coloured colonial. While Kamala Markandaya's *The Nowhere Man* makes the point directly, brutally, and cynically, Anita Desai reinforces the point with subtle irony. Of the two friends, Dev and Adit, Dev appears to be positive, in the sense that he tries to adjust himself to the conditions in which educated Indian immigrants have to survive in England. Adit, on the other hand, is always preoccupied with the problems of arriving at a solution to the problems he visualizes when he goes to India with his English wife, Sarah. Though Adit and Nirode look at the problem of existence from different perspectives, there is a great deal of similarity in their practical approach to the problem. Adit, like Nirode, always indulges in irrelevant talk which is a mild symptom of the wounded self.

In the individual chapters on the writers discussed in this study, the author's intention is to bring to a central focus some of the dominant fictional themes that are unmistakably there in the Indian novel in English. "Self, Family and Society" is neither a theoretical concept nor a sociological principle. It is not employed in the study as a yardstick to measure the success or the failure of the individual novelists or their novels. Since all the novelists under review in this study conform to the conventions of realism and since most of their fictions basically explore the quirks and turns that are common in human relations, the self, the family, and society are used as a theme and variation which have explicatory convenience and exploratory lucidity. One thing that emerges from the study is obviously the variety and the richness that the Indian novel in

English has. The achievement of the individual novelists of this study consists in sensitively responding to the various socio-cultural problems that an Indian has been facing since Independence. The response crystallizes itself into an imaginative construct, the meaning and the relevance of which consist in making sense of modern India, its problems, its people, and its fast-changing socio-cultural milieu.

NOTES

1. Roger Sharrock, *The Figure in a Landscape* (Oxford University Press, 1972). Quoted by Mary Warnock in *Imagination* (London: Faber and Faber, 1976), p. 113
2. Bhabani Bhattacharya, *So Many Hungers!* (New Delhi: Orient Paperbacks, 1978), p. 196.
3. Robert S. Ellwood, "Percival Lowell's Journey to the East," *The Sewanee Review*, LXXVIII, No.2 (April-June 1970), pp. 285-86.
4. John Colmer, *Coleridge to Catch-22: Images of Society* (London: Macmillan, 1978), p. 2.
5. Robert Penn Warren, "The South, the Negro, and Time," in Robert Penn Warren, ed., *Faulkner: A Collection of Critical Essays, Twentieth Century Views* (Englewood Cliffs: Prentice-Hall, 1966), pp. 254-55.
6. Albert Camus, *The Fall,* trans. Justin O'Brien (1957); rpt. Harmondsworth: Penguin, 1972), pp. 86-87.

Bibliography

Primary Sources

Desai, Anita. *Cry, the Peacock.* (1963). Delhi: Orient Paperbacks, 1983.

--------. *Voices in the City.* (1965). Delhi: Orient Paperbacks, 1985.

--------. *Bye-Bye, Blackbird.* (1971). Delhi: Orient Paperbacks, 1985.

--------. *Where Shall We Go This Summer?* (1975). Delhi: Orient Paperbacks, 1982.

--------. *Fire on the Mountain.* New Delhi: Allied, 1977.

--------. *Clear Light of Day.* New Delhi: Allied, 1980.

--------. *In Custody.* London: Heinemann, 1984.

--------. *Baumgartner's Bombay.* New Delhi: Penguin, India, 1989.

Joshi, Arun. *The Foreigner.* (1968). Delhi: Hind Pocket Books, 1972.

--------. *The Strange Case of Billy Biswas.* Delhi: Hind Pocket Books, 1971.

--------. *The Apprentice.* New Delhi: Orient Paperbacks, 1974.

--------. *The Last Labyrinth.* New Delhi: Orient Paperbakcs, 1981.

R.K. Narayan, *Swami and Friends.* (1935). Mysore: Indian Thought Publications, 1944.

--------. *The Bachelor of Arts.* (1937). Mysore: Indian Thought Publications, 1973.

--------. *The Dark Room.* (1938). New Delhi: Orient Paperbacks, 1977.

--------. *The English Teacher.* (1945). Mysore: Indian Thought Publications, 1981. (Published in U.S.A. as *Grateful to Life and Death*).

--------. *Mr. Sampath.* (1949). Mysore: Indian Thought Publications, 1973. (Published in U.S.A. as *The Printer of Malgudi*).

--------. *The Financial Expert.* (1952). Mysore: Indian Thought Publications, 1979.

--------. *Waiting for the Mahatma.* (1955). Mysore: Indian Thought Publications, 1967.

--------. *The Guide.* (1958). Mysore: Indian Thought Publications, 1967.

--------. *The Man-Eater of Malgudi.* (1962). Mysore: Indian Thought Publications, 1973.
--------. *Gods, Demons, and Others.* (1964). Mysore: Indian Thought Publications, 1967.
--------. *The Vendor of Sweets.* (1967). Mysore: Indian Thought Publications, 1967. (Published in England as *The Sweet-Vendor*).
--------. *Reluctant Guru.* New Delhi: Orient Paperbacks, 1974.
--------. *My Days.* (1974). Mysore: Indian Thought Publications, 1975.
--------. *The Painter of Signs.* (1976). Mysore: Indian Thought Publications, 1977.
--------. *A Tiger for Malgudi.* (1983). Mysore: Indian Thought Publications, 1983.
--------. *Talkative Man.* Mysore: Indian Thought Publications, 1986.
--------. *The World of Nagaraj.* London: William Heinemann, 1989.
Rajan, Balachandra. *The Dark Dancer.* (1958). New Delhi: Arnold-Heinemann, 1976.
--------. *Too Long in the West.* Bombay: Jaico, 1961.
Rao, Raja. *Kanthapura.* (1938). New Delhi: Orient Paperbacks, 1971.
--------. *The Serpent and the Rope.* (1960). Delhi: Hind Pocket Books, 1968.
--------. *The Cat and Shakespeare.* (1965). Delhi: Hind Pocket Books, 1971.
--------. *Comrade Kirillov.* New Delhi: Orient Paperbacks, 1976.
--------. *The Chessmaster and His Moves.* New Delhi: Vision Books, 1988.

Secondary Sources

Books

Abbas, Khwaja Ahmed. "Social Realism and Change." *Aspects of Indian Literature: The Changing Pattern.* Ed. Suresh Kohli. Delhi: Vikas, 1975. 145-54.
Anand, Mulk Raj. *Untouchable.* (1935). Delhi: Hind Pocket Books, 1970.
Bande, Usha. *The Novels of Anita Desai.* New Delhi: Prestige, 1987.
Bhattacharya, Bhabani. *So Many Hungers!* (1947). New Delhi: Orient Paperbacks, 1978.

Camus, Albert. *The Fall.* Trans. Justin O'Brien. 1957; rpt. Harmondsworth: Penguin, 1972.

Dhawan, R.K. Ed. *Explorations in Modern Indo-English Fiction.* New Delhi: Bahri, 1982.

--------. *The Fictional World of Arun Joshi:* New Delhi: Classical, 1985.

--------. *The Fiction of Anita Desai.* New Delhi: Bahri, 1989.

Harrex, S.C. *The Fire and the Offering: The English-Language* Novel of India 1935-1970. 2 Vols. Calcutta: Writers Workshop, 1977 and 1978.

Holmstrom, Lakshmi. *The Novels of R.K. Narayan.* Calcutta: Writers Workshop, 1973.

Iyengar, K.R. Srinivasa. *Indian Writing in English.* Rev. ed. New Delhi: Sterling., 1984.

Jain, Jasbir. "Anita Desai." *Indian English Novelists: An Anthology of Critical Essays.* Ed. Madhusudan Prasad. New Delhi: Sterling, 1982. 23-50.

Kanwar, Asha. *Virginia Woolf and Anita Desai : A Comparative Study.* New Delhi: Prestige, 1988.

Kaul, R.K. "The Comic Vision of R.K. Narayan." *Essays Presented to A.G. Stock.* Jaipur: Rajasthan University Press, 1975.

McCutchion, David. *Indian Writing in English: Critical Essays.* Calcutta: Writers Workshop, 1969.

Maini, D.S. "Raja Rao's Vision, Values and Aesthetic." *Commonwealth Literature.* Ed. C.D. Narasimhaiah. Madras: Macmillan India, 1981. 64-89.

Markandaya, Kamala. *A Handful of Rice.* (1966). Delhi: Hind Pocket Books, 1966.

--------. *The Nowhere Man.* (1972). Bombay: Sangam Books, 1975.

Mukherjee, Meenakshi. *The Twice-Born Ficition: Themes and Techniques of the Indian Novel in English.* 2nd ed. New Delhi: Arnold-Heinemann, 1971.

Naik, M.K. *Raja Rao,* Twayne's World Authors Series, 234. New York: Twayne, 1972.

--------. *The Ironic Vision: A Study of the Fiction of R.K. Narayan.* New Delhi: Sterling, 1983.

Narayan, Surendra. "The Ironic Mode of R.K. Narayan." *Indian Writing in English.* Ed. Krishna Nandan Sinha. New Delhi: Heritage, 1979. 169-76.

Narasimhaiah, C.D. *The Swan and the Eagle.* Simla: Indian Institute of Advanced Study, 1969.

--------. *Raja Rao*. Indian Writers Series, Vol. IV. New Delhi: Arnold Heinemann, n.d.

Niranjan, Shiva. "An Interview with Raja Rao." *Indian Writing in English*. Ed. Krishna Nandan Sinha. 19-20.

Parameswaran, Uma. *A Study of the Representative Indo-English Novelists*. New Delhi: Vikas, 1976.

Prasad, Madhusudan. "Arun Joshi." *Indian English Novelists: An Anthology of Critical Essays*. Ed. Madhusudan Prasad. 51-61.

Prasad, Pramod. "The Interaction of Romance and Reality in R.K. Narayan's *The Guide*." *Indian Writing in English*. Ed. Krishna Nandan Sinha. 177-82.

Rajan, Balachandra. "Identity and Nationality." *Commonwealth Literature: Unity and Diversity in a Common Culture*. Ed. John Press. London: Heinemann Educational Books, 1965. Rpt. in *Considerations*. Ed. Meenakshi Mukherjee. New Delhi: Allied , 1977. 1-4.

Ram, Atma, ed. *Perspectives on R.K. Narayan*. Ghaziabad: Vimal, 1981.

Rao, A. Ramakrishna. "The Image of Labyrinth in Borges, Durrell and Joshi." *Glimpses of Indo-English Ficition*. Ed. O.P. Saxena. New Delhi: Jainsons, 1985. III, 13-23.

Sarma, G.P. *Nationalism in Indo-Anglian Fiction*. New Delhi: Sterling, 1978.

Saxena, H.S. "Balachandra Rajan." *Indian English Novelists: An Anthology of Critical Essays*. Ed. Madhusudan Prasad. 62-70.

Sharma, R.S. *Anita Desai*. New Delhi: Arnold-Heinemann, 1981.

Sundaram, P.S. *R.K. Narayan*. Indian Writers Series, Vol. VI. New Delhi: Arnold-Heinemann, 1973.

Walsh, William. *R.K.Narayan : A Critical Appreciation* New Delhi: Allied, 1983.

Journals

Ali, Ahmed. "Illusion and Reality: The Art and Philosophy of Raja Rao." *The Journal of Commonwealth Literature*, No. 5 (July 1968), 16-28.

Anand, Mulk Raj. "The Sources of Protest in My Novels." *The Literary Criterion*, XVIII, NO. 4 (1983), 1-12.

Bhalla, Brij M. "Quest for Identity in Raja Rao's *The Serpent and the Rope*." *ARIEL*, IV, No. 4 (October 1973), 95-105.

Chew, Shirley. "A Proper Detachment: The Novels of R.K. Narayan." *Southern Review*, V, No. 2 (June 1972), 147-59. Rpt. *Readings in Commonwealth Literature*, ed. William Walsh. Oxford: Clarendon Press, 1973, 58-74.

Cronin, Richard. "Quiet Quiet India: The Despair of R.K. Narayan." *Encounter*, LXIV, No. 3 (March 1985), 52-59.

Eng, Ooi Boo. "Making Initial Innocent Sense of *The Serpent and the Rope*." *The Journal of Indian Writing in English*, VIII, Nos. 1-2 (Jan-July 1980), 53-62.

Garebian, Keith. "Strategy and Theme in the Art of R.K. Narayan." *ARIEL*, V, No. 4 (Oct. 1974), 70-81.

Gerow, Edwin. "The Quintessential Narayan." *Literature East and West*, X, Nos. 1-2 (1966), 1-18. Rpt. in *Considerations*, ed. Meenakshi Mukherjee. New Delhi: Allied., 1977. 66-83.

Jamkhandi, Sudhakar Ratnakar. "*The Cat and Shakespeare:* Narrator, Audience, and Message." *The Journal of Indian Writing in English*, VII, No. 2 (July 1979), 24-41.

--------. "Arun Joshi: An Emerging Voice in Indian English Literature." *The Literary Endeavour*, VI, Nos. 1-4, 36-44.

Kaushik, Asha. "Meeting Raja Rao." *The Literary Criterion*, XIII, No. 3 (1983), 33-38.

Kirpal, Viney Pal Kaur. "An Analysis of Narayan's Technique." ARIEL, XIV, No. 4 (Oct. 1983), 16-19.

Krishnamurthi, M.G. "Indian Fiction in English: Some Critical Problems." *Humanist Review*, I, No. 4 (Oct-Dec. 1969), 435-52.

Krishnan, S. "A Day with R.K. Narayan." *Span*, April 1975.

Literary Endeavour, The. III, Nos. 3-4. Special Issue on R.K. Narayan. Guest ed. Vimala Rao.

Mehta Ved. "The Train Had Just Arrived at Malgudi Station." *The New Yorker*, XXXVII, No. 30 (15 Sept. 1962). Rpt. in *John is Easy to Please: Encounters with the Written and Spoken Word*. London: Secker and Warburg, 1971, 133-71.

Nagarajan, S. "An Indian Novel" (a review of *The Serpent and the Rope*). *The Sewanee Review*, XXII, No. 3 (Summer 1964), 512-17.

Narayan, Shyamala A. "Ramaswamy's Erudition: A Note on Raja Rao's *The Serpent and the Rope*." *ARIEL*, XIV, No. 4 (Oct. 1983), 6-15.

Rao, V. Panduranga. "The Art of R.K. Narayan" *The Journal of Commonwealth Literature*, No. 5 (July 1968), 29-40.

Rao, A. Ramakrishna. "Anita Desai's Modernist Novel." *The Literary Endeavour*, II, Nos. 2-3, 11-14.

--------. "Kirillov in The First Circle." *The Literary Endeavour*, VI, Nos. 1-4, 45-54.

Satapathy, S.C. "From Passivity to Awareness: A Study of the Narrator-Protagonist in Arun Joshi's *The Apprentice*." *Journal of Literary Studies*, II, No. 2, (December 1978), 121-31.

Sharrad, Paul. "Aspects of Mythic Form and Style in Raja Rao's *The Serpent and the Rope*." *The Journal of Indian Writing in English*, XII, No. 2 (July 1984), 82-95.

Shastri, N.R. "*Where Shall We Go This Summer?*: A Critical Study." *Osmania Journal of English Studies*, XVII (1981); 83-103.

Updike, John. "R.K. Narayan, a Writer Immersed in His Material." *Span*, April 1975

Venkatachari, K. "R.K. Narayan's Novels: Acceptance of Life." *Osmania Journal of English Studies*, VII, No. 1 (1969), 51-65.

--------. "Raja Rao's *The Serpent and The Rope:* A Study in Advaitic Affirmation." *Osmania Journal of English Studies*, VIII, No. 1 (1971), i-xii.

Walsh, William. "The Intricate Alliance: The Novels of R.K. Narayan." *A Review of English Literature*, 11, No. 4 (October 1961), 91-99.

--------. "Nataraja and the Packet of Saffron: The Indian Novel in English." *Encounter*, XXIII, No. 4 (October 1964), 78-83. Rpt. *Readings in Commonwealth Literature*, ed. William Walsh. Oxford: Clarendon Press, 1973. 51-57.

General

Anderson, Quentin. *The Imperial Self.* New York: Alfred H. Knopf, 1971.

Booth, Wayne C. *A Rhetoric of Irony*. Chicago: The University of Chicago Press, 1974.

Bradbury, Malcolm. *Possibilities: Essays on the State of the Novel.* London: Oxford University Press, 1973.

--------, and McFarlance, James, ed. *Modernism: 1890-1930.* Pelican Guides to European Literature. Harmondsworth: Penguin, 1976.

Chidbhavananda, Swami, trans. *The Bhagavad Gita:* "Introduction." Tirupparaitturai: Tapovanam, 1965, 1-65.

--------. *Facets of Brahman Or The Hindu Gods.* Tirupparaitturai: Sri Ramakrishna Tapovanam, 1971.

Cohn, Dorrit. *Transparent Minds: Narrative Modes for Presenting Consciousness in Fiction.* Princeton: Princeton University Press,

1978.

Colmer, John. *Coleridge to Catch-22: Images of Society.* London: Macmillan, 1978.

Coomaraswamy, Ananda K. *The Dance of Shiva.* Bombay: Asia, 1956.

Gokak, V.K. *The Concept of Indian Literature.* New Delhi: Munshiram Manoharlal., 1979.

Goodheart, Eugene. *The Failure of Criticism.* Massachusetts: Harvard University Press, 1978.

Halperin, John, ed. *The Theory of the Novel: New Essays.* New York: Oxford University Press, 1974.

Hartman, Geoffrey. *Beyond Formalism: Literary Essays 1958-1970.* New Haven: Yale University Press, 1970.

Hynes, Samuel. *The Auden Generation: Literature and Politics in England in the 1930s.* London: The Bodley Head, 1976.

Josipovici, Gabriel. *The World and the Book: A Study of* Modern Fiction. Frogmore: Paladin, 1973.

Kawin, Bruce F. *The Mind of the Novel: Reflexive Fiction and the Ineffable.* Princeton: Princeton University Press, 1982.

Kennedy, Alan. *The Protean Self: Dramatic Action in Contemporary Fiction.* London: Macmillan, 1974.

Leavis, F.R. "Sociology and Literature," *The Common Pursuit.* 1952; rpt. Harmondsworth: Penguin, 1976.

Lubbock, Percy. *The Craft of Fiction.* 1921; rpt. London: Jonathan Cape, 1965.

Nisbet, Robert. *Sociology as an Art Form.* New York: Oxford University Press, 1976.

Nalbantian, Suzanne. *The Symbol of the Soul from Holderlin to Yeats.* London: Macmillan, 1977.

Rockwell, Joan. *Fact in Fiction: The Use of Literature in the Systematic Study of Society.* London: Routledge and Kegan Paul., 1974.

Scholes, Robert and Kellogg, Robert. *The Nature of Narrative.* New York: Oxford University Press, 1966.

Stern, J.P. *On Realism,* Concepts of Literature. London: Routledge and Kegan Paul., 1973.

Sypher, Wylie. *Loss of the Self in Modern Literature and Art.* New York: Random House, 1962.

Watt, Ian. *The Rise of the Novel: Studies in Defoe, Richardson and Fielding.* 1957; rpt. Harmondsworth: Penguin, 1963.

Other Works Cited

Alexander, Peter, ed. *William Shakespeare: The Complete Works.* 1951, rpt. London: Collins, 1960.

Borges, Jorge Luis. "Everything and Nothing" and "The House of Asterion." Trans. James E. Irby. *Labyrinths: Selected Stories and Other Writings.* 1964; rpt. Harmondsworth: Penguin, 1981. 170-72 and 284-85.

Eliot, T.S. "East Coker." *Four Quartets.* 1944; rpt. London: Faber and Faber, 1959. 231-32.

Ellwood, Robert S. "Percival Lowell's Journey to the East." *The Sewanee Review*, LXXVIII, No. 2 (April-June 1970), 285-309.

Forster, E.M. *A Passage to India.* 1924; rpt. Harmondsworth: Penguin , 1972.

Hess, Robert.D. and Handel, Gerald, "The Family as a Psychological Organization." *The Psychological Interior of the Family*, ed. Gerald Handel. Chicago, 1967.

Krishna Murthy, M. "The Harijan." *The Peacock Lute: Anthology of Poems in English by Indian Writers*, ed. V.N. Bhushan. Bombay: Padma, 1945, 73.

Lawrence, D.H. "The Novel." *Phoenix II: Uncollected, Unpublished, and Other Prose Works by D.H. Lawrence,* ed. Warren Roberts and Harry T. Moore. 1968; rpt. New York: Penguin, 1978. 416-26.

Prabhavananda, Swami and Isherwood, Christopher. Trans. *The Song of God: Bhagavad-Gita.* New York: The New American Library, 1954.

Sharrock, Roger. *The Figure in a Landscape.* Oxford University Press, 1972.

Warren, Robert Penn. "The South, the Negro, and Time." *Faulkner: A Collection of Crritical Essays.* Twentieth Century Views. Robert Penn Warren, ed. Englewood Cliffs: Prentice Hall, 1966. 251-71.

Wordsworth, William. "Rob Roy's Grave." *The Poetical Works of Wordsworth.* Eds. Thomas Hutchinson. Rev. ed. Ernst D. Selincourt. 1936; rpt. London: Oxford University Press, 1959. 231-32.

Other Works Cited

Index

Indian Society for Commonwealth Studies

Chairman	*Exec. Chairman*	*President*
Dr. Mulk Raj Anand	Prof. Sudhakar Pandey	Prof. Chaman Nahal

The ISCS is an all-India academic organization that aims at promoting Commonwealth Literature including Indian English Literature. To promote wider interest in Commonwealth Literature, the Society proposes to (1) organize or sponsor talks, discussions, seminars and symposia (II) bring out a newsletter every fourth month (III) publish or sponsor publication of bulletins, catalogues, bibliographies, monographs and books (IV) publish/ sponsor publication of a research journal on Commonwealth literature (V) recommend delegates for international seminars (VI) set up Centre for Commonwealth studies with the facility of a library for the members. Amongst its other activities of promoting awareness, scholarship and mutual understanding, the Society organizes an annual national/international convention on a specific literary theme. The participation is limited strictly to the ISCS members and other special invitees.

The first annual convention was held at the University of Poona on 27, 28, 29 January 1989. The second annual convention was held at S.K. University, Anantapur, 22-24 March 1990. In each of these conferences, about 150 scholars from India and abroad participated in the deliberations. The next annual conference will be held at the Department of English, Utkal University, Bhubaneswar. Tentatively on 28-30 January 1991. All ISCS members are invited to participate. The delegation fee of Rs 150 towards accommodation and hospitality may be sent by Money Order/ Demand Draft to Ms. Seema.

ISCS MEMBERSHIP SUBSCRIPTION

Membership is open to anyone in India and abraod interested in Commonwealth Literature.

Life	Rs. 500	U.S.$ 200
Institutional	Rs. 1000	U.S.$ 300

Life membership subscription may be sent by M.O./D.D. Cheques of Rs. 515 (including bank charges) should be made in favour of **Indian Society for Commonwealth Studies.** Institutional members will be entitled to receive publications of the Society including notices, bulletins, Newsletters, copies of the journal. Crossed cheques may be sent even by ordinary mail. All Correspondence may be addressed to: Ms. Seema, Executive Secretary, ISCS, C-129, Mansarovar Garden, New Delhi 110 015.

THE COMMONWEALTH REVIEW

A bi-annual of creative and critical writing

Articles on Indian writing in English and other Commonwealth literatures are invited from the ISCS members. Manuscripts should be neatly typed in double space. References should as far as possible be incorporated into the text of the article. Footnotes, which should be functional, should follow the MLA stylesheet. Contributions to the journal and books for review (two copies each) should be sent to: Ms. Seema, Secretary ISCS, C-129, Mansarovar Garden, New Delhi 110015

Subscription Rates

	Individuals	**Institutional**
Each Copy:	Rs. 40	Rs. 50
Annual:	Rs. 75	Rs. 100
3 Years:	Rs. 200	Rs. 250
Life (Non-recurring):	Rs. 500	Rs. 1000

Members will receive the publications of the Society free of charge. The last issue of **The Commonwealth Review** was on Salman Rushdie Scholars/teachers are requested to send orders on behalf of their institutions.

Call for Papers

The forthcoming issue of the **Commonwealth Review** will be a special number on **Australian Literature and Indian Literature: Studies in Mutual Response**. Papers from Indian scholars on Australian literature and from Australian scholars on Indian literature are invited. Last Date: 15 September 1990.

The January 1991 issue of the **Commonwealth Review** will be a special number on **New Zealand Literature**. Papers should be sent by 15 December 1990 to the ISCS Secretary.

Rohit Dhawan

J-391, New Rajinder Nagar
New Delhi: 110 060
Ph: 5737849

Rajat Dhawan

J-391, New Rajinder Nagar
New Delhi: 110 060
Ph: 5737849

(Dr.) R.K. Dhawan
J-391, New Rajinder Nagar
New Delhi 110 060
Phones: 5737849 (6.30-8.30 a.m.
9.30-11 p.m.)
5507139 (5-8 p.m.)

(Dr.) R.K. Dhawan
(Dr.) Usha Dhawan
J-391, New Rajinder Nagar
New Delhi 110 060
Ph. 5737849